GERALD BRENAN

Thoughts in a
dry season

A MISCELLANY

CAMBRIDGE UNIVERSITY PRESS

CAMBRIDGE

LONDON · NEW YORK · MELBOURNE

Published by the Syndics of the Cambridge University Press
The Pitt Building, Trumpington Street, Cambridge CB2 1RP
Bentley House, 200 Euston Road, London NW1 2DB
32 East 57th Street, New York, NY 10022, USA
296 Beaconsfield Parade, Middle Park, Melbourne 3206, Australia

First published 1978

Printed in Great Britain at the
University Press, Cambridge

ISBN 0 521 22006 8

CONTENTS

Foreword vii

Life 1

Love 14

Marriage 29

Death 34

Religion 39

Art and
architecture 62

Literature 82

Writing 115

Ying Chü 121

People 127

Nature 133

Places and
peoples 150

Introspection 163

Dreams 168

To Theodore Redpath

I love anecdotes. I fancy mankind may come
in time to write all aphoristically, except in
narrative: grow weary of preparation and
connection and illustration and all those arts by
which a big book is made.

Dr Johnson, from Boswell's *Journal of a Tour
to the Hebrides*

THOUGHTS IN A DRY SEASON

Tenants of the house,
Thoughts of a dry brain in a dry season.
T. S. ELIOT, *Gerontion*

FOREWORD

For many years I have kept a notebook in which I jotted down odd thoughts or aphorisms that came into my head as well as short passages that struck me from the books I was reading. Then in 1972 I had the idea of copying them out and arranging them in sections according to their subject. This suggested to me the possibility of extending them to form a book in which I could record some of the thoughts and observations that occurred to me, so I began to add new ones and omitted most of the quotations. I ended by adding so many that the new entries outnumber the old ones by at least thirty to one and are often much longer.

Since it seemed best to avoid too great a uniformity of style and because some subjects called for a more prolix treatment than others, I varied my manner as the book went on and relied less on apophthegms, while in the last sections I added a few pieces that are more personal.

At the last moment it has been necessary to omit five of the original sections of this book – those on philosophy, history, society, politics and revolution, as well as certain entries on poets – because its length was already too great and the costs of publishing have risen very steeply. I mention this because it explains what the reader may feel as gaps in the text.

Some of these little pieces contradict one another since I am apt to think differently at different times, and indeed am capable of thinking opposite things at the same time, but I have made no attempt to rectify this because my instinct has been to write honestly according to my feelings at the moment rather than to put forward a consistent view. The general cast of my mind inclines me to a moderate scepticism, hostile to cant and dogmatism, and to believing that whatever opinions we have should be held with humility. For this reason I make no claim to truth or justice for any of these little pieces, however dogmatic their tone may appear to be. Let the reader take them as he wishes. All I have aimed at has been either to provoke thought or to entertain, and if I have sometimes succeeded in this I shall be satisfied. I would further like to say that I am very conscious of my inadequacy to deal with some of the subjects that are included in this miscellany. I was never at a university and can claim no special knowledge of anything. All my life I have been a learner rather than a knower, a dabbler in matters that were often beyond my natural range or capacity, so that when I treat of these I can only excuse myself with the hope that in an age of specialists the approach of an amateur may have some interest. I have my intuitions – that is all.

I planned this book to suit many different tastes and fancies, to be opened at hazard and skipped rather than to be read right through. Some sections I wrote for my friend Cyril Connolly, whose books I greatly admire and to whom I sometimes sent things that I had written. But he has died. Since then I have felt that I was writing chiefly to satisfy a wish to empty my mind of some of the casual accumulations it had acquired in the course of years – in other words, to finish reaping my field. Had I begun it ten years earlier it would have been a better book, for when one passes eighty only the crumbs of one's mental faculties are left. But it is the fate of all writers to regret the books they have not written or have begun to write when it was too late. What they succeed in getting down in the course of their lives is, or so they feel, only the tip of an iceberg.

I would like to express my thanks to my friend Dr Theodore Redpath of Trinity College, Cambridge, for his great kindness in reading through the first half of this book in manuscript and writing comments on it at a time when he was very busy with his own things. Other friends – Frances Partridge, William Byron and Frederick Wildman – have also been kind enough to read some of these sections and to give me their advice. But my chief thanks are due to Lynda Nicholson Price for going through each section of this book as I wrote it: her help and advice have been invaluable to me.

January 1977

Life

‡ The life of man from his conception to his death may be compared to the course of a train which, starting at express speed, gradually slows down and stops. In the first months of his existence he passes through the stages that his ancestors took millions of years to travel: then he explores new territory, after which all his efforts are turned on the last few miles of his course. How far will he get before he is stopped?

‡ We must assign to progress, if it exists, something more than the accumulation of knowledge and technical capacity. To be of value it must mean an improvement in our dealings with other men and in the rational enjoyment of leisure. Yet as soon as a new stage in this is reached fresh obstacles appear, so that for every step forward a step or half a step is taken back.

‡ 'Every man believes in his youth,' said Goethe, 'that the world really began with him and that everything exists merely for his sake.' From this belief come all the problems of adolescence.

‡ The ambitious man looks back on his life as the racing driver does on his last race, going over in his mind each lap and corner and considering how much better he might have taken it if he had changed down sooner, braked later and so forth. These thoughts of 'If only...' are the chief occupation of his old age.

‡ 'Men are like wine,' said Cardinal Roncalli, later Pope John XXIII, to Herriot. 'Some turn to vinegar, but the best improve with age.' He also said to Herriot, who was an atheist or agnostic, 'After all the only thing that separates us is our ideas – c'est à dire, très peu de chose.' If only for his exquisite manners he deserves to be canonized.

‡ *Introspection.* When one turns a microscope onto a piece of cloth, one no longer sees cloth but something different. So it is when one looks into oneself. Things keep their character and identity only when they are seen on the scale that is appropriate to them.

‡ When we find that we are giving several different explanations of our conduct, we know that we are concealing something from ourselves.

‡ The things we are best acquainted with are often the things we lack. This is because we have spent so much time thinking of them.

‡ When we see other people's silliness we forgive ourselves our own silliness and when we see our own silliness we forgive that of other people.

‡ By courage is meant the power to resist one's enemies. By moral courage that to resist the pressures of the crowd and sometimes those of one's friends.

‡ There is black and white malice and black and white envy just as there is black and white magic. White malice and white envy have no hatred in them and so hurt no one. Indeed they add a spice to conversation.

‡ Sometimes we plan our unhappiness with the same zest with which we plan our happiness. Is that because in planning we get a release of energy?

‡ There is nothing so exhausting as making decisions. Napoleon's greatness lay in his being able to make them all the time on a large variety of matters and usually correctly.

‡ He has had a life of struggle and frustration and is not happy. I have had little struggle and am happy, so that there is a gulf between us. For the unhappy both envy and despise the happy: it's almost a class distinction.

‡ I often have generous impulses, but they are usually followed by mean or prudential ones. These last are worth at least £200 a year to me.

‡ There is hardly any act so base that I cannot imagine myself committing it if the pressure of circumstances imposed it on me. One only has to be sufficiently frightened or jealous or angry to know that one is capable of almost any bad action, especially if it could be done in secret. Or if not actually committing it, then wishing to commit it.

‡ Men would like to love themselves, but they usually find that they cannot. That is because they have built an ideal image of themselves which puts their real self in the shade.

‡ We confess our bad qualities to others out of fear of appearing naïve or ridiculous by not being aware of them.

‡ We soon cease to feel grief at the deaths of our friends, yet we continue to the end of our lives to miss them. They are still with us in their absence.

‡ Intellectuals are people who believe that ideas are of more importance than values. That is to say, their own ideas and other people's values.

‡ There are some sorts of illusion which it is harmful to hold and others which are helpful. Let us at least preserve our idols.

‡ Hypocrisy occurs when one can't admit to what one really feels. Thus class feeling and colour prejudice are present in most people, but have to be disguised.

‡ Some people think before they speak. Others speak first and are often surprised by what they hear themselves say. These are the intuitive.

‡ Poverty is a great educator. Those who have never known it lack something.

‡ There is something the poor know that the rich do not know, something the sick know that people in good health do not know, something the stupid know that the intelligent do not know.

‡ Wisdom means keeping a sense of the fallibility of all our views and opinions and of the uncertainty and instability of the things we most count on.

‡ People often speak with greater conviction when they are lying than when they are speaking the truth. Is that because they are more enamoured of what they have so cleverly concocted than of what merely chanced to happen?

‡ Memory is not so much the repository of the things we wish to remember as the trick of laying our hands on them whenever we want them. We have all the books we require in our library but cannot find where that urgently needed one was put.

‡ A bad memory is the mother of invention. Shakespeare, who could put his finger on every word and adage in the English language, forgot all the Latin he had learned at school.

‡ We all of us carry about with us a secret enemy who hides our pencils, our spectacles, our air tickets and that important business letter we have to answer at once. He goes everywhere with us, a silent poltergeist, whose sense of humour we never learn to appreciate.

‡ We aim at happiness, but when we look back over the years we find that what we have gained has been experience. In this, says Schopenhauer, we are like the alchemists, who failed in their aim of making gold but discovered instead far more valuable things such as gunpowder, medicines, new chemical compounds and some of the laws of Nature.

‡ Happiness requires as one of its constituents the feeling of permanence: the belief that this or something like it will go on forever.

‡ Sometimes the knowledge that there is just one disapproving puritan in the world, looking out from his belfry, is enough to destroy our pleasure.

‡ Vicky O'Rourke's parties. The boredom and misery of the well-to-do is more poignant than that of the poor because it is a sign of the poverty of their natures and so is incurable. The poor at least know what they want.

‡ Some men live alone in order to forget themselves. It is the presence of other people that reminds them, often painfully, of their own inadequacies.

‡ The frog eats, sleeps, digests and lays its eggs at the bottom of the pool and only rises to the surface to communicate with its fellows. So it is with writers, painters and composers.

‡ 'He who lives in the society of men cannot be visited by angels' (St Martin of Tours).

‡ Poverty is the cure for certain kinds of guilt. When I was young and very poor I looked everyone in the face and felt free.

‡ For the young poverty can be an adventure, as they know that they will come out of it, but for the poor it is a routine.

‡ Accompanying all our best and most disinterested acts there is a tinge of self-esteem and self-congratulation. It is as if a little monkey were riding on a horse and gesticulating, 'Look at me. I am riding on this horse. It is *my* horse. It is *I* who am riding it.'

‡ When we admire someone we like to hear him praised by others – but not too much.

‡ According to Seneca we are greedy of our money but spend-thrift of our time, although that is the only thing we ought to be careful of. But this is the view of an ambitious man, for most people live in order to kill time.

‡ We are only intermittently alive. In habit, which takes up a large part of our existence, we re-enact the dead substance of our past living experience. That is to say, habits are our mental bones, without which neither we nor society could get along.

‡ We are closer to the ants than to the butterflies. Very few people can endure much leisure.

‡ Three quarters of the meanness of the rich is due to their fear of being thought mugs. For every rich man feels that he is occupying a fortress which is besieged by those who want something out of him.

‡ *Platonic types.* The Platonic type or idea of each of us, towards which we tend, sits behind the high brick walls of the county lunatic asylum. Paranoiacs, schizophrenics, melancholics, manic depressives, people who believe they are God or the Emperor Napoleon, people who sit motionless like statues, people who move about all the time, people who suffer from a total recall of memory, people who never stop talking – among them we see our purified images, our completed models. As we grow older we come to resemble them more closely because with the failure of our energies we are forced to contract into ourselves and so to become our own essences. If we do not join them it is probably because we have furnished our own private asylum for ourselves.

‡ Normality is a happy balance of qualities like the white light which contains hidden within it all the colours of the spectrum. It helps us to adjust ourselves to other normal human beings, but disqualifies us from understanding or sympathizing with those from whom some of the bands of the spectrum are missing.

‡ Most of our personal opinions lie on the board like iron filings. But pass the magnet of a strong emotion over them and they will change overnight and point in the opposite direction.

‡ We make the same mistakes again and again and blaming ourselves does not always, as we hope it will, prevent us from repeating them. For these mistakes come from some flaw in our nature.

‡ We can feel ashamed for our parents or for our wife or husband because we imagine that their gaffes or crudities reflect on us, but the person we most often feel ashamed of is ourselves. There we go again! Sometimes we feel like mothers carting about with them children who are continually disgracing themselves in public.

‡ We ask what we are to do about all these distressing things – our inadequacies and our problems and our failures. But there is nothing we can do about our lives except live them.

‡ The more we feel sorry for ourselves, the less sorry others will feel for us. People don't waste their small store of sympathy on those who can provide it so richly for themselves.

‡ Everyone is a bore to someone. That is unimportant. The thing to avoid is being a bore to oneself.

‡ We may think we know ourselves well, but there is always something we don't know and that is the thing that stares other people in the face.

‡ Everyone alters and is altered by everyone else. We are all the time taking in portions of one another or else reacting against them, and by these involuntary acquisitions and repulsions modifying our natures.

‡ We may think that we love our friends, yet none of them completely satisfies us. They have sides that jar on us while we have sides that meet with no response from them. Not one of them could we live with. How strange then and how miraculous that we can happen on persons of the opposite sex with whom we can communicate wholly and entirely down to the last nook and cranny of our being. Love, that all-dissolving fire from heaven, brings about this union of incompatibles, and though the physical side will nearly always have its role to play, in the long run it is less decisive than is commonly imagined. For love is a mental thing which in its craving for complete fulfilment makes use of bodily union to replenish its reservoirs.

‡ The best kinds of friend are those whom one can tease. In every close relationship there should be room for a little playful showing of the claws, if only to prove that we can bridge our differences. Therefore no standing on dignity.

‡ The art of politeness and good manners is that of concealing our own egoism and pandering to that of others. We please best

when we draw people out and get them to shine, better still to talk of themselves.

‡ Exaggeration weakens what we say though it is intended to strengthen it. Properly speaking it is one of the weapons of satire and fantasy, but when used straightforwardly it is a mark of lack of self-confidence.

‡ There are people who think that truth is more important than life. These are the pedants, for the truth, if taken too narrowly, can be the enemy of life, as every anthropologist and psychiatrist knows. Leave people their harmless illusions.

‡ What every generation forgets is that their children are going to react against the ideas and values in which they have been brought up. Thus the children of dogmatic atheists are apt to become Wesleyan missionaries, those of enlightened liberals to opt for Communism, those of the very rich for Trotskyism and those of Communists for Catholicism. So the world changes.

‡ The new ideas of one age become the ideologies of the next, by which time they will in all probability be out of date and inapplicable.

‡ When we see the prejudices and oddities of our friends we realize that we are that rare thing, a perfectly sane and normal person. But strange to say our friends do not agree with us.

‡ In complete sanity there is always a certain element of denseness and complacency. It is a country of the mind that calls up Denmark – flat and dull. Or does it consist rather of a balance of neuroses, hidden under a mask of conformity?

‡ 'Do you want a man who is sane and sound-minded, do you want one who is steady and well ordered in his ideas? Then muffle

him in ignorance, in idleness and sluggishness. We must stupefy ourselves to become wise and dazzle ourselves to find our road' (Montaigne, *Essays*).

Montaigne, in spite of his own very great intelligence, distrusted those who lived too much by the intellect because he thought that it prevented them from understanding either life or people. Pascal read this passage and turned it to his own purposes. There is something both innocent and dead about those who live solely by the reason.

‡ 'The admission of women to complete equality with men would be the most certain mark of civilization: it would double the intellectual forces of the human race and its probabilities of happiness' (Stendhal, *Rome, Naples, Florence*). Men have taken a long time to realize that they will get more pleasure from women's company by treating them as equals in education and in everything else than by confining them to the role of housewives and concubines.

‡ Quality is an aristocratic thing, quantity a democratic one. We most of us want to be aristocratic in taste and in our love of the best, but the times are against us. Today the only aristocracy is that unseen one of the intelligent and the discriminating – that is, of those who are addicted to the things of the mind not for their utility but solely for their own sake.

‡ As Coleridge said, 'We receive but what we give.' The happy life is a life of continual generosity in which we go out to meet and acclaim the world.

‡ One road to happiness is to cultivate curiosity about everything. Not only about people but about subjects, not only about the arts but about history and foreign customs. Not only about countries and cities, but about plants and animals. Not only about lichened rocks and curious markings on the bark of trees, but about stars and atoms. Not only about our friends but about that strange labyrinth we inhabit which we call ourselves. Then, if we do that, we will never suffer a moment's boredom.

‡ We should live as if we were going to live forever, yet at the back of our minds remember that our time is short.

‡ Cruelty is regarded by most people today as an outrage against human nature, yet this is quite a modern sentiment. Almost alone in past ages Montaigne singled it out as the greatest of vices, saying that he hated it 'both by instinct and by reason'. He deplored it not only when it was practised upon men, but upon plants and animals. Two centuries later he was followed by Voltaire in his campaign against *l'infâme*. Yet there has never been an age, not even the Dark Ages, that has seen more cruelty than ours.

‡ There are times when the sight of a blackbird in the jaws of a cat can set off a painful stream of thought which carries us far afield. Life, we then say to ourselves, is a tragedy, though our complacency and addiction to pleasure will most of the time prevent us from realizing it. But if one day our good fortune fails us, our eyes are opened and we say with Chamfort that in our passage through life 'il faut que le coeur se brise ou se bronze' – the heart must either break or become as bronze. Chamfort, who was a liberal, cut his throat to avoid being guillotined by Robespierre.

‡ For the same reason that soldiers in a battle cannot afford to let themselves be affected by the sight of the dead and the dying, so we dare not let ourselves be too wrought on by the terrible things that happen around us in the world. We have only so much sympathy to give and that makes us resemble those Indian Brahmins who pass calmly on their way through streets filled with the sick and dying. There are so many of them and their misery is so extreme and so irremediable that these superior men would destroy themselves if they stopped to sympathize with them. Lord Shaftesbury was an exception, a rich man who was nauseated by bad smells and sordid conditions, but whose conscience would not let him rest so long as such misery existed close to him. But then he was that rare thing – a Christian who tried to follow the teaching of the Gospels.

‡ Reality – that's what we have to live with. And one part of reality is our own nature and its limitations. We must take in as much of it as the poverty of our natures will allow.

‡ In pleasure we luxuriate in the present. In pain we live in the present too, but retreat into our own body. Pain becomes our universe and to cope with it we try to become our pain and to acquire its rhythm and pulsate with it. For if we are our pain, we cease to be ourselves.

‡ He saw the familiar things that had hitherto seemed to him almost part of himself – the table, the window, the chest of drawers – suddenly cut off from him. *They* did not feel his pain, *they* had no connection with him. His life was concentrated here within his body. 'Je souffre,' he said to himself, 'donc je suis.'

‡ In pain it is as if someone rang the doorbell and it would not stop ringing, but went on and on. 'All right. I hear you. I'll go to the dentist. As soon as he can see me.' But the bell has gone mad and will not stop.

‡ R. tells me that she heard B. saying to himself, 'I hate my children, I hate everyone.' After sixty, people enter on an un-mapped territory. All sorts of unconscious fears, hates and passions lie in wait for them as well as the first symptoms of new illnesses. Their night thoughts invade their day ones. Yet few writers have described these people. In novels we rarely find anyone over sixty who is not a fossil, though the growing of a shell may be merely a means for protecting a stormy inner life.

‡ The chief vices of the elderly are dogmatism and complacency, which are a sort of rheumatism of the mind brought on by long-continued habits. The chief vices of the young are gullibility and fanaticism, which are due to the fact that, being new to life and inexperienced in its problems, their idealism revolts against the world in which they find themselves and which they suppose has been created by the greed and stupidity of their elders.

‡ Old age takes away from us what we have inherited and gives us what we have earned.

‡ In many old men there is a King Lear, waiting for the moment to break out.

‡ *The pessimism of the old.* 'And Joseph brought in Jacob his father, and set him before Pharaoh...And Pharaoh said unto Jacob: "How old art thou?" And Jacob said unto Pharaoh: "The days of the years of my pilgrimage are an hundred and thirty years: few and evil have the days of the years of my life been, and have not attained unto the days of the years of the life of my fathers in the days of their pilgrimage"' (Genesis 47.7).

‡ *Promises and memories.* The beauty of gardens, of lilac, of perfumes; the moonlight, the wind in the pine trees, the cuckoo calling and the owl hooting. When we are young they intoxicate us with their promises, they tell us that this is our own true country in which we shall always be travelling. But when we begin to grow old they speak to us of the past and of the days which we will never, *nunquam, jamais, jamás* see again.

Love

‡ We are aware that falling in love is the commonest thing in the world, occurring even among birds and animals, and so we observe it among other people with little interest. But when it happens to us for the first time we feel it to be something inexplicable and miraculous such as can never have happened before to anyone.

The overwhelming nature of this experience is due to the fact that it comes from the merging of two egos. The great forces locked up in self-love are released and directed upon someone else. What was static before becomes kinetic. But this is not how it appears when it happens. A person falling in love for the first time has the sensation of being taken over by some new and unknown power whose existence he had not previously been aware of. The fables of ancient deities such as Venus and Cupid come into his mind, for he knows that by himself he could never have arrived at such a pitch of feeling. If he is honest he will see that the intensity of his state is out of all proportion to the merit or love-provoking qualities of the object. But honesty is not a thing he is likely to have much use for.

At first the realization of what is happening to him may lead to some alarm and apprehension. He finds himself being swept away into a fathomless gulf, into a loss of self where anything may happen to him. At each moment a new vista, so that by the end of a week he has the sensation of having lived through a year. But then the speed becomes less rapid, the movement less dizzying. A new world looms out of the mist where everything is delicate and magical.

‡ One of the more notable consequences of falling in love is the annihilation of everything in the lives of the lovers that had taken place before their meeting. This is natural, since with their discovery of one another they have been born again. As Donne wrote:

> I wonder by my troth, what thou and I
> Did, till we lov'd? were we not wean'd till then?

So they begin a new history. From now on every event in their shared life will be recorded, every detail pored over, while to celebrate these occasions imaginary plaques will be put up on the sites of their first glances or kisses. Then whenever their early past is discussed, 'what you were doing at the time when I was doing that' is the form it takes, since it is impossible that they could ever have been together in the same world without there being some secret and occult connection between them. Destined from the beginning to come together, there must always have been signs of that future in each of them.

‡ Lovers, as everyone knows, live wrapped up in one another, oblivious of the rest of the world, exalted high above its ordinary occupations, in a state of mutual entrancement and ecstasy, yet such is the potential of this current set up between them that some of its energy is spilt over onto other things. The lover then sees the force that has taken possession of him operating through the whole of Nature. The songs of the birds, the flowering of the plants are a part of it. Love, which for Dante moves the stars, is moving everything.

The greater richness of his effective life makes him sensitive to poetry: he not only reads it but for the first time in his life he writes it. All his faculties are extended so that, in spite of the nervous exhaustion his state brings, he feels himself to be living on a higher intellectual and spiritual level than previously. It is as though he had discovered a secret staircase leading up from the basement on which he had previously dwelt to an upper floor. There, out of the window, he has a view of the fields and hills that before were hidden from him.

‡ One of the great things about falling in love is that it is involuntary and effortless. It is like sliding down a gentle slope on a toboggan.

‡ It is best to wade in slowly, to savour every moment, for it is the first moments that will be the best.

‡ 'There is not a limb nor a muscle in my body that does not represent to me the pleasure I find in being with you' (Henri IV, *Letters*).

‡ One of the most subtle pleasures of love is the feeling it gives of collusion. The two lovers are standing together against the world.

‡ The best thing in love is tenderness.

‡ Absence and letters are the forcing ground for love. What renews it and confirms it is presence and bed.

‡ Some people seem to fall in love instantly, in a flash, but the ground has always been unconsciously prepared beforehand. No one falls in love against his wishes, however disastrous to the rest of his life the consequences may be.

‡ 'I cannot live with you – that would be life' (Emily Dickinson).

‡ When the coin is tossed, either Love or Lust will fall uppermost. But if the metal is right, under the one will always lie the other.

‡ Many lovers believe that there are mysterious correspondences between themselves and their loved one. They attach importance to the fact that they were born in the same month, share the same initials, have each a mole on their side, dislike oysters, have a horror of shoelaces, cannot do accounts. Their differences they call complementary.

‡ Lovers like to believe that there is some special affinity between them which has been responsible for bringing them together and which makes them so right for one another. Their friends only notice that they have fallen for the first more or less suitable person that came to hand.

‡ In love we discover the good qualities of our loved one which are hidden from other people. 'How can she love that dolt?' her friends ask. But she has found under his oafish exterior secret qualities that charm her. One of these qualities is his passion for her, since a large part of love is an exercise in mutual flattery.

‡ According to La Rochefoucauld the pleasure of love lies in loving and we are made happier by that than by being loved back. That is to say, loving someone else relieves us of some of the weight of our self-love.

‡ 'The reason lovers and their mistresses are not bored by one another's company is that they talk all the time about themselves' (La Rochefoucauld).

‡ There are people who imagine that they are in love with one another because they wish to be in love with someone. Between them they blow up a bubble and each is surprised when it suddenly collapses and bursts.

‡ Love can be no more than the conspiracy of two people to live at a more rapid rate, in a more highly charged atmosphere, at a superior level to the rest of the world. This allows them to feel that they are a little nobler, a little more genuine than their friends.

‡ We are not always as much in love as we think we are.

‡ Men have different tastes in most things, but incline to the same taste where women are concerned. That is, they are all drawn to a pretty face and a good figure. Yet if a man could be attracted to

plain women, he would have a wide choice and no competition, as well as deep gratitude from the one whom he had picked on.

‡ Ugliness in men is not necessarily a disadvantage to them. Although some women must have good-looking lovers because that flatters their self-esteem, most prefer vitality and character.

‡ Women are very critical of their own sex and look at them more often in the street than they do at men. They are also more aware of their own requirements, so that in love it is always they that take the first step. They know that they are the magnets and, if they are flirts, turn on and off their spell as it pleases them.

‡ In women's eyes men are the innocent sex. They lack antennae. They can take in a simple situation, but rarely know what is going on round them.

‡ Each sex has a role marked out for it. As Nell Dunn says, men are always trying to assert themselves, while women are chameleons and like to play the role men throw on them. Yet it is usually the women who control the situation.

‡ Vanity often plays a large part in love-affairs. Men who consider themselves good in bed will be drawn to women who have had many lovers, in the hopes of proving to them that they can make love better. For the same reason timid men will avoid them since they will fear any comparison.

‡ Women are not as a rule afraid of men whom they know, yet many men are afraid of women. The documents of the past fifteen hundred years provide plenty of evidence of that. Is this because men feel themselves to be clumsy and helpless in dealing with creatures who are emotionally and socially more mature than they are?

‡ In the case of a man who is deeply in love and is going to bed with his girl for the first time, this fear may show itself in an attack of impotence. How to approach her with the same crude procedures that he has tried out on women of no importance? According to Stendhal, these fiascos were common in his time because then the most desirable women were ladies, wrapped in an aura of inaccessibility, or else actresses possessing a certain prestige, but they still occur today in normal men because love and admiration often precede sexual attraction. They may even exclude it.

‡ But women also have their problems. Thus making love to a girl for the first time can be like going into a dark room and fumbling for the electric switch. Only when a man has found it will the light come full on.

‡ Books on sex describe for their readers a hundred or more body positions. But in love there are hundreds of thousands of psychological positions and these each couple has to work out for themselves.

‡ Many men and women who regard themselves as normal cannot bring themselves to the act of love unless a spice or savouring is added. Thus some, as in *Lady Chatterley's Lover*, have to begin by repeating obscene words, others need to quarrel, others to laugh all the time, others to have a tap running in the bedroom. I know of a man who could not make love to the young girls he fancied unless a Mozart record, always the same one, had been put on. Something of the same sort is to be found among birds. Chaffinches, for example, find a long ritual of courtship necessary, and if a single item is bungled or omitted they must stop and start again from the beginning. Since copulation is the most important act in the lives of living creatures because it perpetuates the species, it seems odd that Nature should not have arranged for it to happen more simply.

‡ Some men like to think of love-making as a form of aggression and cannot embark on it without a show of violence. So too

many women get a thrill from imagining that force is being used against them. But when it is actually used they hate it.

‡ Sexual perversions are as infectious as venereal disease and are passed from one person to another. This is especially true of sado-masochism.

‡ Women forget that when they take an ugly or unprepossessing lover they lose much of their own attractiveness in the eyes of other men because some of his qualities will seem to have rubbed off on them. So the wise husband exercises a censorship on his wife's lovers.

‡ Some girls only fall in love with ugly men. These are the girls who when they were children preferred golliwogs to dolls.

‡ Men who marry girls but fail to satisfy them sexually often end by bearing a resentment against them. It is their male pride which has suffered, for men have more pride about their sexual prowess than they have about their charm or their good looks, and so they pay off on their partners their shame at their failure.

‡ Whenever they were in bed together and he failed to come up to scratch she felt as badly let down as when her car refused to start. Resentment, followed by indignation.

‡ He sometimes regretted that he was not living in an age when running away from women was regarded as a mark of Christian virtue.

‡ There are people who think of love-making as an exercise in the worship of the human body. They regard it as a religious cele-bration which has a ritual of its own and concludes with an act in which each partakes of the substance of the other.

‡ 'It takes a hundred times more intelligence to make love than to command an army' (Ninon de Lenclos (1620–1705), a famous courtesan at the court of Louis XIV).

‡ The importance attached today to skill in love-making has been greatly exaggerated. Spontaneity is everything. That is to say, sexual converse ought to proceed like verbal converse with mutual give and take.

‡ 'Nothing is so varied in nature as the pleasures of love although they are always the same' (Ninon de Lenclos).

‡ Sexual adventures are a game like tennis or ping-pong for filling in our leisure. But love is an intensified form of life.

‡ What happiness can be compared to the happiness of returned love? Yet it is very precarious. As plants exhaust the minerals they need in the soil and die, so love consumes the substances it lives on. Then the desire for new partners sets in.

‡ *Winter thoughts.* He thought of the bodies of young women as bees think of the corollas of flowers which they will visit when the warm weather returns.

She thought of male bodies as the anenomes think of the furry bumble-bees who will arrive some sunny morning and ruffle their pistils and stamens.

‡ Women's bodies – is there anything in the world more absorbing? Some men like to adventure in remote parts of the earth, exploring the stony deserts or the silent rain forests, but for others it is women's bodies that hold the greatest mystery. Every inch of them, every mole, every crease, every freckle. There are even those who would like to take Alice's diminishing medicine and then be swallowed by the loved one so as to discover what she is like inside.

‡ It is usual today to think that sex is enjoyable, but this has not always been the case. There have been ages, such as the early Christian one, when it was so strongly charged with shame and disgust that many people were glad to escape from it. Traces of this feeling still linger on with us, for sex that has not been re-processed by love is an ambiguous affair and apt to be followed by a reaction. Indeed it is not impossible, so some people tell us, that such a reaction is prepared to break out today in the form of a total reversal of our present permissive attitudes. Capitalist society, they point out, has grossly overemphasized the pleasures of sex because money is to be made out of it, whereas a collectivized society that takes its ideology seriously is likely to reduce it to its biological role and frown on anything that, by pandering to the private tastes of the individual, will distract him from carrying out his duties to the community, which alone matter. In a totally collectivized society such as that of the ants, sexual union is sup-pressed altogether, or rather confined for the sake of procreation to a couple of individuals. But this is the extreme state or Utopia, when social life reaches its perfect fulfilment, and it is not to be supposed that human beings are sufficiently altruistic to be capable of achieving it.

‡ Those who have some means think that the most important thing in the world is love. The poor know that it is money.

‡ In Mediterranean countries love is compelled to develop slowly because the chastity required of unmarried girls prevents consum-mation. So lust or liking grows into love because it cannot attain its object. This gives time for the consolidation of the lovers' relation so that it often ends in a happy marriage.

‡ In northern countries young lovers begin by going to bed. Then Eros takes over till the freedom of choice and abundance of oppor-tunity bring the affair to an end and set off another one. Love in modern cities is thus a sort of musical chairs, but with higher stakes and forfeits than most of the players wish for.

‡ In the past, when courtships were tepid, angry fathers, jealous husbands or dangerous illnesses were required to start a great passion. Today one just steps into the maelstrom and is carried away.

‡   En la orillita del mar
            Suspiraba una ballena.
            Y en sus súspiros decía,
            'En amor hay siempre pena.'

            On the edge of the sea a whale lay sighing.
            And among its sighs it said – 'In love there is always
            pain.'
            (A popular Spanish *copla*)

‡ One May day in Tuscany a girl hears a blackbird singing of love in the orchard. 'O bird from Florence, tell me how love begins.' And the bird answers, 'Love begins with songs and carols and ends with pain and weeping. Love begins with carols and songs and ends with tears and pain' (A. d'Ancona, *Poesia populare fiorentina nel secolo XV* (1862)).

This song is a *rispetto toscano* or *strambotto* of the fifteenth century. Most medieval songs put into the mouths of women strike this note.

‡ At the beginning of every love-affair one may often see the fault on each side which will in the end wear it down and destroy it. Sometimes the first quarrel will bring it out.

‡ Some quarrels end in greater estrangement, others in reconciliation and bed. One must acquire a knack for quarrelling as huntsmen and jockeys acquire a knack for falling without hurting themselves.

‡   The white stone on the beach grows no lichen:
            So love without quarrels has no savour.
            (A modern Greek distich)

‡ In fading love-affairs some people quarrel solely for the sake of the reconciliation which will reassure them that they are still in love.

‡ In love-affairs that are not going well it is often important to have a confidant. Things look less important when they are put into words.

‡ In difficult love-affairs, where one loves more steadily than the other, stability can best be maintained by treaties. It is true that these treaties will not be kept, that every few months they will be broken and replaced by others, but still they provide a breathing space. Lovers, like nations, must seek for interludes in their perpetual warfare.

‡ The world has always approved of great passions even when they ran contrary to its moral code. In the splendid language of the medieval ballad of Conde Claros: 'Que los yerros de amores – dignos son de perdonar' – 'faults of love deserve to be forgiven.'

‡ Some people take a pride in being unhappily in love because they consider that the strength of their feelings ennobles them and raises them above the common herd. Thus Hazlitt in his book *Liber Amoris* wrote an account of his violent but unrequited passion for his landlord's commonplace daughter. Its key phrase is: 'I am in some sense proud that I can feel this dreadful passion – it gives me a kind of rank in the kingdom of love.' He showed his pride by publishing his book during his lifetime.

‡ The reason why people persist for years in a hopeless passion is often that they do not want to be cured of it because they feel themselves incapable of sustaining a requited love.

‡ 'Into a well from which you have drunk cast no stone' (The Talmud).

‡ There is a stage in dying love-affairs when the keenest pleasure one can find lies in giving pain because the remorse that will follow will rekindle one's love.

‡ In love one becomes cruel. 'His only wish now was to attach her more closely to himself in order then to give her pain by throwing her over. To make *her* suffer a little he was ready to suffer a hundred times as much himself.'

‡ The dark side of love is jealousy, which can be either rational or irrational. It is rational when we have good reason for thinking that all we have in life is at stake.

‡ Do not believe those persons who say that they have never been jealous. What they mean is that they have never been in love.

‡ Jealousy is like a black cloud that spreads over the sky and turns all our thoughts and feelings to its own colour. Then suddenly, for no apparent reason, the cloud blows away and we find it hard to believe that it ever existed. 'I was not myself,' we say.

‡ One of the torments of jealousy is the uncertainty. Has she been to bed with him or not? Then search her letters to find out. The first victims of this disease are mutual trust and confidence.

‡ Books, places, amusements, people – how meaningless they become when we suspect that the person we love loves someone else!

‡ Jealousy revives and stimulates our love while at the same time it poisons it. But it alienates the loved one by showing her the limits of her freedom and setting up in her feelings of guilt which will make her wish to escape.

2   BTT

‡ Always the same dreary thoughts, always the same futile plans, always the same useless regrets. In such cases the mind becomes an automaton. What escape can there be?

‡ In dressing, in shaving, in every little act that he performed he felt a force drawing him back, a kind of resistance or friction which said, 'Why do this?' He could not answer, and the pain he felt and was unable to get rid of attached itself to these trivial actions and made it appear that it was they that were hurting him and not the fact that she had left him.

‡ We show ourselves at our worst when we are jealous. Our long lugubrious faces, our suspicious manner, our anger or sulkiness repel the person we wish to please. The line connecting us with her is broken and we can no longer talk freely.

‡ There are three forms jealousy can take: hatred of the rival, hatred of the loved one and hatred of oneself. The last case shows itself in the wish to eliminate oneself, to cease to exist, to disappear. It is a sort of schizophrenia.

‡ The person who causes jealousy feels no sympathy or compassion for the person who suffers it, but only resentment for this attack on his or her freedom.

‡ We laugh at the jealousy of our friends though we would not laugh at their toothaches or arthritis. Yet jealousy can be more painful than these.

‡ We are ashamed of being jealous and try to hide it because the fact that we have a reason for it offends our pride. Indeed three quarters of our jealousy comes from wounded pride.

‡ The jealous man or woman lives in a vacuum. None of his friends will tell him what he most wants to know.

‡ Jealous people always act contrary to their own interests. They know it, but cannot help it.

‡ Jealousy either numbs or it releases energy. The wild or violent acts committed by the people who have been hurt in love are not so much due to their wish to repay as to their absolute need for taking action.

‡ In Mediterranean countries jealousy among men is retrospective. They want to marry not merely a virgin but a girl who has never been kissed. The women on the other hand are proud of their lover's previous conquests, so that if he has not had any he will be obliged to invent them.

‡ How ineradicable is egoism! When we are in love we imagine that we have uprooted it entirely and put all our heart and effort into pleasing and procuring the happiness of another person. Then jealousy looks in at the window and our self-regard returns.

‡ In love we breathe and feel through the medium of another person. When she leaves us our life is over till there has been time for new organs to grow.

‡   Caeli, Lesbia nostra, Lesbia illa,
        illa Lesbia, quam Catullus unam
        plus quam se atque suos amauit omnes,
        nunc in quadriuiis et angiportis
        glubit magnanimi Remi nepotes.

        O Caelius – my Lesbia, that Lesbia, that same Lesbia whom Catullus loved more than himself and all his dear ones, now in the crossroads and alleys tosses off the spawn of lordly-minded Remus.
        (Catullus, *Carmina*)

‡ Under all this, under the hold she exerted over him, the nice words that he found himself saying to her, the kisses they exchanged,

there was a lower floor from which unspoken words of a different nature emerged – 'Whore, fraud, liar! Go away. I'm through with you. I loathe you.'

‡ 'Ciascun si fascia di qual c'egli è inceso' – 'Everyone swathes himself with that which burns him' (Dante, *Inferno* XXVI).

Marriage

‡ '*Amicitia* is love whose object is not *what* one desires, but the person *for whom* one desires good. It is in marriage that the greatest *amicitia* should exist' (St Thomas Aquinas, *Summa Theologica*).

‡ The qualities required for a good marriage are more substantial than those required for a love-affair. They involve every aspect of the personality, so that when physical attraction declines the marriage will remain as firm and as well grounded as ever.

‡ According to La Rochefoucauld there are good marriages but no delicious ones. In his time marriage was an institution that did not begin with falling in love but grew into it, if at all, gradually. Today love comes first, yet even so a violent infatuation is not the best presage for connubial stability.

‡ The great thing about marriage is that it enables one to be alone without feeling loneliness.

‡ Marriage is a steady state which picks up its own fuel as it goes along and so renews itself.

‡ In a happy marriage it is the wife who provides the climate, the husband the landscape.

‡ Married love is a stream that, after a certain length of time, sinks into the earth and flows underground. Something is there, but one does not know what. Only the vegetation shows that there is still water.

‡ The movement of her hands, twined together and swollen from chilblains, gave him a feeling of pity. He pitied not her but those twining childlike hands. No, he would never be able to leave her.

‡ After the death of a husband or wife the survivor is apt to feel remorse, not so much on account of things said or done as because of failures of love.

‡ There is a disease which attacks marriage as a mildew attacks plants. This is a sullenness or resentment that settles on the feelings and if not arrested will spread through the system and poison its smallest thoughts. Very trivial things can bring it on, but with the passage of time they are apt to accumulate until a long list of petty grievances has been drawn up. The only cure lies in having a quarrel in which everything is brought out and aired, the end coming in reconciliation and bed.

‡ She got to know his conversation so well by heart that talking to him was like reading last week's newspaper.

‡   When the rainë raineth and the goosë winketh
      Little thinketh the gander what the goosë thinketh.
      (Medieval proverb)

‡ Marriage is an arrangement by which two people start by getting the best out of one another and often end by getting the worst.

‡ Marriage is like a railway train. It can only leave the rails if there is an accident.

‡ Very small things can wreck a marriage. It can be enough if one partner likes to sleep with the window open and the other with it closed.

‡ Middle-aged couples who are bored with one another will find that they draw closer together if they keep a dog. Or better two dogs, one for each.

‡ Lack of means is one of the chief things that holds marriages together. The couple cannot afford to separate. Then, after the children have grown up, there is the fear of loneliness.

‡ When married women want a flutter but are afraid of becoming involved in a love-affair they choose a house painter or a window cleaner or else a foreigner they have met on holiday, because then there will be no risk of its lasting.

‡ One of the most tiresome things about the presence of a female friend or relative with a married couple is that she tends to get caught up in the ebb and flow of the magnetic current that binds them. She never understands what is going on because she brings her moral judgements to bear on them. Is she kind to him? Is he considerate to her? And so on. She forgets that there is a thread of masochism and sadism, of attraction and resentment, running through most marital relations and that this thread may be stronger than many thicknesses of well-intentioned rope. Marriage in fact is the best protected secret there is, and those who attempt to intervene or take sides are likely to find themselves out in the cold when they least expect it.

‡ Cupboard love is not to be despised. Although women need to be loved for themselves, men who have passed fifty feel more secure when they are loved in large part for their bank balance. As a rule their modesty is not misplaced.

‡ When one of the partners in a marriage reproaches the other for concealing things from him or even for lying, he has as a rule only himself to blame. He had allowed himself to become a person to whom it was not easy to confide or to speak the truth.

‡ For some men marriage is the cradle of egoism, for in it they expect perfection in the woman who has the honour to be married to them, while they themselves feel free to do as they please. 'Darling, this soup is disgusting.'

‡ A good reason for marrying Spanish women rather than English ones is that they are satisfied with their sex and have no feelings of inferiority about it. They will not therefore make one suffer because there have as yet been no women Shakespeares or Miss Cézannes.

‡ Some people can only criticize their husband or wife in the presence of visitors. They do it in a jocular tone but there is often feeling behind what they say.

‡ The girl who holds feminist views vows herself to independence. No man, she says, will ever turn her into a house-slave and so prevent her from fulfilling herself as an artist or writer. But then she gets married. Subjugated by the pleasures she finds in that state, she is now ready to shop, cook, sew and type for her partner, and her career as a painter or writer is postponed and finally forgotten. This happens because love is usually a much stronger and deeper thing for women than it is for men. They fulfil themselves in it, in their care for their husband, their home and their children, whereas for men it is merely the background to their real life, which lies outside the house in their work. That is the principal reason why married women have up to the present occupied a subordinate position in the arts. They are the generous sex, men the egoistic one.

‡ The Moslems have always treated their wives as objects of great value who must be kept locked up like jewellery. We think it

strange that these women were pleased by this, but till European ideas began to affect them they felt flattered by it. The slightest relaxation of the rules on the part of their husband offended them because it seemed to show that they were not appreciated by him at their true value. For which of the two sexes, one may ask, was married life the more onerous?

Death

‡ When we are young and in good health we sometimes enjoy thinking about death. Doing so gives us a pleasant thrill, but we are not deeply affected, because we cannot believe that we shall ever cease to exist. Death is for other people, not for ourselves.

‡ Speaking generally, death is natural and the friend rather than the enemy of life. We have only to imagine its not existing to see that this is so. All right, agreed – yet in our particular case we want it postponed for as long as possible.

‡ 'A life with no death in it, with no katabolism in its incessant anabolism, would be no more than a perpetual death, a forced repose. Real life is maintained by death' (Miguel de Unamuno).

‡ For some people the idea of death is a sauce that gives a savour to life. They have to challenge it from time to time in order to get the full sensation of being alive.

‡ Some people love death as one loves one's mistress. 'Dear beauteous death, the jewel of the just.' They can play with it, stroke it, fondle it and do everything they please with it except look it in the eyes. For then they would see that it doesn't exist, but is merely a name for the cessation of life.

‡   Come lovely and soothing Death,
      Undulate round the world, serenely arriving, arriving,
      In the day, in the night, to all, to each,
      Sooner or later, delicate Death.
      (Walt Whitman, *When lilacs last in the door-yard bloom'd*)

‡ 'For we needs must die and are as water spilt on the ground, which cannot be gathered up again' (II Samuel, 14.14).

‡ *The ship of Charon.* 'A ship full of young people has put out to sea: at the stern are the sick, at the prow are the wounded and under the sails those who have been drowned at sea. It seeks a port to enter, a haven to rest in; at last in a good harbourage it drops anchor. And the rumour goes out among the villages: "Widows, they are selling your husbands; mothers, they are selling your children and you, poor sisters, they are selling your brothers." The mothers hurry down to the port with florins, the sisters with presents and the widows, the wretched widows, with large keys in their hands; and those who have nothing with joined hands.

'But all at once Charon changes his mind and cuts the cable. And the mothers recross the mountains, the sisters the slopes of the hills, and the widows, the wretched widows, the solitary valleys.' (A dirge-like poem from Epirus, from *Chansons populaires grecques*, collected by Emile Legrand, 1876)

In modern Greek folklore Charon is not the ferryman over the Styx, but Death himself. Yet his boat remains, for he is represented as putting into port with his load of drowned and dying and then, after refusing the supplications of their families, sailing off again. In a rather confused way, for it had come down orally, this lament conveys the grief and despair of these very poor peasants who have lost their sons who were also their breadwinners. Through all Greek folk poetry there runs a deeply tragic note that is not found in other folk poetry, except in some ballads.

‡ David's lament for his son Absalom who had rebelled against him and been executed contrary to his wishes: 'O my son Absalom, my son, my son Absalom! Would God I had died for thee, O Absalom, my son, my son!'

‡ When we pass fifty every gust of wind brings round the bend of the river the sound of the waterfall that our canoe is approaching.

‡ We should live as if we were never going to die, for it is the deaths of our friends that hurt us, not our own.

‡ It is when we lose someone we love that the idea of death first begins to bite. Apart from our grief, the grim accessories rise up and afflict us – the alteration in the corpse, the consignment to the ground, the worms and the decay and the final grinning skeleton. Yet these things have nothing to do with the human creature who has died, but are rather a mockery of her. Death is a jester and we should refuse to be taken in by the profanities he offers us.

‡ When last Christmas I looked up 'Death' in my dictionary I found only a few lines. Now I see whole pages on which are written the most deeply graven memories of my life. (April 1932)

‡ Mr Canning, an old sailor who had done odd jobs for me in the garden, was buried today. I had meant to go to his funeral, but at the last moment could not bring myself to do so. When we attend the funerals of our friends we grieve for them, but when we go to those of other people it is chiefly our own deaths that we mourn for.

‡ At the funerals of our relations we do our best to put on long faces, but at the luncheon afterwards our hilarity breaks out. For it is he who has died and not ourselves.

‡ The most beautiful cemetery in the world is that of Savannah in Georgia. Here the old grey tombstones set in green grass are shaded by live oaks that are hung with long strands of grey, weeping, Spanish moss. In such places death seems both poetical and natural.

‡ When Walt Whitman worked as a male nurse in the hospitals of the Civil War he wore a flower in his button-hole and a smile on his face, and the sight of his gaiety cheered up the wounded and the dying.

‡ 'To accustom yourself to death I find you need only draw closer to it' (Montaigne, *Essays*).

‡ The old rarely fear death since they live at its doorstep, but they often feel apprehension about the terminal illness. Will it come in fire with agonies of pain or as a stroke that paralyses them and leaves them dependent on other people? It is one of the hypocrisies of our age that doctors are not allowed to practise euthanasia.

‡ No one has ever recorded the sensation of dying. According to Italo Svevo it is like having an orgasm. All the forces of the body and mind gather together and pour themselves out in one tremendous convulsion.

‡ Death, as the biologists tell us, came into the world with sex and each of these contains some portion of the other. It is thus the price we pay for love, since the amoeba lives for ever because it propagates itself by division. In a certain sense we do this too when we give parts of ourselves to our lovers and friends.

‡ 'Your death is a part of the natural order of the universe...It is the condition of your creation, it is a part of yourself. In fleeing from it you are fleeing from yourself' (Montaigne, *Essays*).

‡ We do not completely die if we have loved, for by the act of loving some part of us passes into the loved person or object. Trees, hills, fields, all the life of Nature, then poetry, music, painting, our friends, our dear ones and our country. In the course of loving these we give some portion of ourselves to them and

that portion, which is the best we have, survives us. This is our immortality, or at least our gradual transition to that state of not-being when the nebulae pass beyond the range of telescopes. For something tells us in our clearer moments that we do not live for ourselves alone but are links in a chain, items in an unfolding pattern, and that at least a part of such significance as we have depends on the significance of the whole. By our love we accept and take to ourselves a portion of that whole, thus becoming a larger self which will survive us. As Ezra Pound said, in one of the most beautiful passages of English poetry:

> What thou lov'st well remains,
> > the rest is dross
> What thou lov'st well shall not be reft from thee
> What thou lov'st well is thy true heritage
> (*Pisan Cantos*)

‡ O death, where is thy jolly old sting? as Bertie Wooster said when his Aunt Agatha died leaving him a cool fifty thousand.

Religion

‡ When Hiero, the Greek tyrant of Syracuse, asked the poet Simonides of Ceos to explain to him the nature and attributes of God, he begged to be given a day in which to consider the question. When this had elapsed he asked for two days more, and so on, doubling the period every time. On Hiero's expressing his astonishment at this procrastination, Simonides replied that the longer he thought about the matter the more obscure it became. Cicero, who tells this story in his *De natura deorum*, agrees with him.

‡ 'God saw everything that he had made, and behold, it was very good' (Genesis 1.31). This is the foundation of Western religion. The afterthought that it is not after all so very good leads to theology.

‡ The greatest danger to human life lies in a sense of its triviality. It was this that brought down Rome and that may one day bring down the United States and Russia. One of the merits of Christianity has been its insistence on the importance of every moment.

‡ 'To propose to Man no more than what is human is to betray him, to will his unhappiness, for by the principal part of himself, the spirit, he is called to something greater than a merely human life' (Jacques Maritain, *Humanisme intégral*). But what is meant by a merely human life, seeing that religion is a creation of humanity?

‡ Christian dogma is a myth and it is being rapidly eroded by another myth – that the scientists know or soon will know all the answers. This last, though it does not place any strain on our credence, is in every way less suited to the requirements of human life and culture. So what are we to do? Human beings demand to be told that life has a purpose and the scientists either say nothing about that or affirm dogmatically that it has none.

‡ Everyone who believes that life has a meaning believes in God, whether or not he uses these words to express it. Yet can there be a meaning in life unless we ourselves have put it there? That is to say, only our conscious or unconscious faith can give us one. Science and reason will never tell us.

‡ 'God is to the Universe what the laws of stress are to a bridge' (Spinoza). We say that we believe in the laws of physics, though a scientist will tell us that these laws have no real existence, but are merely shorthand expressions to describe the way in which certain things happen. But suppose we took up a different position and said, as Plato would have done, that these laws have a greater reality than the events they govern. We should then be nearer to understanding what Spinoza meant.

‡ The word that most needs explaining today in the context of religion is 'belief' or 'faith'. Many people suppose that believing in the existence of God is the same sort of thing as believing in the existence of Australia: if true, it should be capable of proof. Yet we believe that some poets and composers are better than others and, though we can give good general reasons for this being so, we can never prove it in any particular case. We have to be attuned to their particular idiom before we can acquire our certitude about it, just as some people will claim that one has to be attuned to the presence of God and feel him drawing us before we can believe that he exists. Yet we must not whittle down this word 'faith' by analogies, for it is a very positive thing. Thus we may feel attracted to the religion and cult of Apollo, but we cannot, try as we will, believe in his existence.

‡ The question is asked, 'Does God exist?' But God does not exist in the same way as do those things which form the objects of experience for our natural faculties. For those who have a sense for him, he exists or rather subsists, to use the technical theological term, on an entirely different plane and is apprehended in another manner. To the mystic or the totally believing person this is an apprehension of universality and certitude: a presence as pervasive as the ether which the scientists used to postulate, and of such authority and importance that beside it nothing else matters.

‡ It will be said that few of those who profess faith in God have this direct experience of him. They are those who believe on hearsay. They find the hypothesis of his existence plausible and so construct round it their life-pattern of rites and observances and moral conduct. These are the conventional believers who find support for their faith in the beliefs of their parents and neighbours.

‡ When a man asks whether there is any objective truth in religion he is asking the wrong question. What he should ask is, 'What need does it answer? Does it enlarge and strengthen our lives? Has it a natural root in the depths of our being?'

‡ 'Even if God did not exist, religion would still be holy and divine. God is the only being who, in order to reign, need not exist' (Baudelaire, *Journaux intimes*).

‡ Children when they read fairy stories can both believe and not believe at the same time. So can primitive men. So often did the Elizabethans. But since the steam-roller of rationalistic thought has passed over us we cannot do this, which means that we have lost one half of ourselves. We are so intent on being adult that we have forgotten our childhood.

‡ The people who really believe in God are the people who feel a need for him. In the smug, comfortable West religious faith has declined, but in Russia today it is different. There, we are told,

the churches are crowded and not only with the elderly. In spite of the anti-God propaganda put out by the state and of the obstacles raised against church attendance, between thirty and fifty million people regard themselves as believers. All the great Russian poets and writers of this age have been Christians. When everything else has been taken from a man all he has left is God.

‡ 'Protagoras taught that man is the measure of all things, and so abolished the sense of a "beyond" which gave Greek thought its driving impulse and sense of direction' (Maurice Bowra, *The Greeks*). Without that sense of a beyond there is always something petty about men's affairs.

‡ It could be said that the words 'believing in God' convey little more than a certain way of orienting one's life. They offer a signpost, pointing out the road to be followed. The young migrating bird has no picture in its mind of what lies at the end of its journey. Or if it has such a picture it is likely to be a false one.

‡ No doubt the so-called truths of Christianity are, objectively speaking, illusions. No doubt, as Freud says, God is a sublimation of the child's father. But can men live without illusions? If they do not have one they have another and it can at least be said of this one that it will never let them down. Yet is not a belief in God something much more than an illusion? It gives a form and content to an appetence that is felt by many people and which needs to be satisfied if they are to live to full capacity. When one considers what the great religions have done to build up and hold together society and to tame the greed and the violence of men, one may well regret their decline.

‡ 'Sancho's faith is a real faith, fed on doubts. For genuine faith is maintained by doubt. Only those who doubt can believe' (Unamuno in his book on *Don Quixote*). This is not true, but doubt can produce a tension that will increase the wish to believe and lead to a sort of agony if one cannot. This seems to have been the situation of Unamuno, who longed to believe because he

could not bear to think that his life would end in extinction. In his *New York Letter* Auden speaks of 'our life well balanced by our doubt'.

‡ 'Neque enim quaero intellegere ut credam, sed credo ut intellegam.' 'Nor do I seek to understand that I may believe, but I believe that I may understand. For I know that unless I first believe I shall not understand' (St Anselm). Faith must come first. In the first book of his *Confessions* St Augustine questions this.

‡ A feeling for religion gives a greater depth to life, so that it is not surprising that nearly all the greatest minds of the past have been religious. Yet wishing to believe does not help one to do so. In the climate of today there has to be some deep and strong emotional pressure before it can come about. And even if there is this pressure, it may express itself in atheism, as it did with Lucretius, but an atheism that shows a profound religious concern.

‡ One would expect Christianity to be rejected by nearly all educated people because in the context of the modern world it is obvious nonsense. 'Credo quia absurdum est' – 'I believe because it is absurd', is not a normal person's attitude, but the intellectual pervert's cry. And the degree of its absurdity has grown since Tertullian's time. Yet it has been the religion of nearly all Europeans during the past sixteen hundred years and still retains a strong unconscious influence on our thinking and feeling. Its poetry and painting find a willing reception in our minds and almost all our moral ideas are derived from it. It would seem only reasonable therefore to maintain some sympathetic link with it and on the proper occasions to allow oneself the right to poetic belief.

‡ 'Offer sacrifices to the Spirits as though the Spirits were present' (Confucius).

‡ 'If the sun and moon should doubt they'd immediately go out.' So Blake. For faith is the biological force that carries us foward,

together with all living things, and makes us point hopefully in the direction of the future. Such is natural faith, without which it is hard to live, whereas religious faith is a canalization of this in a certain direction and for certain ends. Belief in God begins inside us like hunger for food, but it leads outside us to where the food lies. The desired end (and some mystics have said the whole process) is known as God and every believer envisages him according to the kind and degree of his mental faculties and upbringing. That is to say, faith is founded on an inner experience, but what that experience entails will be differently described by each person. Believers, unless they accept a conventional formula, differ as much from one another as do philosophers. The only thing on which they agree is a feeling of certainty.

‡ There is a God of metaphysicians and a God of churchgoers. They do not appear to be the same person. But is there a word in the language that is capable of being interpreted in so many different ways? It is a portmanteau word from which everyone will unpack the meaning and image that suits him.

‡ Some people have too much natural faith to belong to any religion. They believe as the animals do, because faith in the future is implanted in them as an instinct.

‡ Sartre and Camus both declare that life is absurd. The foxes and birds, which have a much harder struggle to survive, do not appear to think so. But men frequently lose their zest for life when the conditions become too easy, and ask of it more than it can give them.

‡ Religious dogmas are often expressed in the form of paradoxes. As a rule they record moments in the development of a religion when important choices had to be made, so that to grasp their relevance one must go back to the historical circumstances under which they arose. Thus the Athanasian Creed or *Quicunque vult* is a signpost put up at a fork in the road to show the way that had to be taken. The point at issue, which was the relation between

the Three Persons of the Trinity, may seem to us meaningless, but a different choice would have led to very different historical results. The leaders of the Church were steering the car of Christian ideology, just as Lenin was later to steer that of Russian Communism.

‡ Theology is like algebra – that is, a way of manipulating terms you don't understand. These terms are codifications of religious attitudes, if not symbols of occult power.

‡ 'A creed gives expression to a definite collective belief, whereas the word religion expresses a definite subjective relationship to certain metaphysical, extramundane features' (Jung).

‡ Myths are attempts to give expression to collective experience in poetic form. In their imagery and symbolism they have many analogies with dreams.

‡ Religions are kept alive by heresies, which are really sudden explosions of faith. Dead religions do not produce them.

‡ The reason why in past ages heretics and atheists had to be put down is that religious faith is such a precarious thing, so exposed to the bacillus of doubt, that complete assent to it by the whole community was needed to maintain it. For the chief reason for believing an improbable story will always be that everyone round us believes it too.

‡ *Original sin.* This doctrine, conveyed in the Babylonian myth of the expulsion of Adam and Eve from Eden, expresses what Catholics call the radical insufficiency of man. He is not and never can be perfect. However much he aspires to a Utopia or Promised Land, he will never reach it. The Hebrew prophets, including Jesus, did not accept this, for they believed in the advent of a Messiah who would set up the Kingdom of God on earth. Nor did Marx. But this hopeful view has faded except among the

young. Today it would seem to be the mark of maturity of mind
to believe that men must continue to the end of time to hate and
kill one another and make a desert of the world they live in. We
have read too much history to think otherwise.

‡ God maintains his hold on man by promising him things. The
beauty and pathos of the Book of Deuteronomy derive from his
many-times-repeated promises, which one knows will not be fulfilled, or will be fulfilled only in a devious and long-deferred way.
In some parts of *Paradise Lost* Milton shows himself very sensitive
to the tone of these passages.

‡ 'Fecisti nos ad te et inquietum est cor nostrum donec requiescat
in te.' 'Thou hast created us for Thyself and our heart cannot be
quieted until it rest in Thee.' These words of St Augustine from
the first pages of his *Confessions* express the loneliness felt by the
educated men and women of his age, lost in the great, aimless,
philistine world of the late Roman Empire with its love of blood
and its coarse pleasures and its decaying vitality. The close, vital
world of the Greek cities as well as the tribal world of the Italian
communities had long vanished and left behind them a great
emptiness. The earth had lost its attractiveness and only the
spiritual values offered by religion remained.

‡ St Peter Damiani, mystic and theologian of the eleventh century,
said that God could make what had happened not to have happened.
This notion of the all-powerfulness of God is really a Moslem idea
and when taken literally makes history and science impossible.

‡ When life was harsh and cruel the gods were cruel too. There
was no Gentle Jesus in the Dark Ages. He was the ruthless judge,
casting down sinners into hell. As life became easier this severity
was mitigated, the doctrine of Purgatory was defined and the
Virgin was brought forward as an intercessor. So it was not, as
is said in Genesis, God who created man after his image, but the
other way round.

‡ *Cosmic despair.* When I was a boy and was told that some day the sun would grow cold and all life on the earth come to an end, I felt that it was not worth living any longer. So it happened with many Victorians when Darwin proved that the story of Adam and Eve was a myth. One recovers.

‡ God is always being made. Just as man, according to the existentialists, makes himself by his choices and decisions, so he makes his god to provide him with the guidance and encouragement he needs. I here, God there – it's a simple view suited to simple people. But the less simple find that, as Jesus said, God is also within them.

‡ Moral ideas are rationalizations of instincts that have been built into human beings and animals and developed by tradition and upbringing. Everyone who has kept cats or dogs knows that they have a moral sense and feel guilt when they fail to live up to it. This sense, as it is developed in men, becomes first the tribal law and then the voice of conscience.

‡ *Tertullian and the Montanists* (*c.* A.D. 200). After every revolution there comes a moment when it has to be decided whether the revolutionary enthusiasm is to be kept up or whether it should be encouraged to settle into fixed and stable forms. Tertullian joined the Montanist sect in Asia Minor because he wanted to keep the spirit of early Christianity alive by means of free prophecy and glossolalia (the 'gift of tongues') which came directly from the Holy Ghost, and not let it harden into Church government and ritual. Compare Mao and the Cultural Revolution.

‡ 'During the Christmas vacation...the discussion turned on ethics. Wittgenstein thought "the good is what God commands" preferable to "God wills the good because it is good"' (from a review in *The Listener*, 8 August 1968) of *Ludwig Wittgenstein und der Wiener Kreis*, notes of Wittgenstein's talk recorded by F. Waismann).

‡ What a relief on reading the Old Testament to find none of that nonsense about God being good in the moral sense! Just as he has given the sheep their law and the lions their law so he

has given men their law, which it is their life to keep. But he himself does not keep it, he is beyond it and above it, and that is why many religious people find relations with him so difficult.

‡ God is the power that ordains and reassures. Why then all these undeserved calamities? Various answers to this question have been given: 1. They *are* deserved, since Adam's guilt has been inherited by his descendants; 2. They are there to strengthen and purify us; 3. God sees the whole, we see only the part; 4. All will be well in the end because our sufferings will be made up to us in a future life. I do not accept any of these answers.

‡ To Tennyson the ruthlessness to be found in Nature, the eating and being eaten, was the chief obstacle to a belief in God. But if one sees Nature as a process in time and living creatures as links in a chain, where is the problem? For it is the chain that matters.

‡ A certain Moslem Sufi said that it is as absurd to regard God as being just or as having moral attributes as to regard him as having hands and feet. One must not see him in anthropomorphic terms; yet, if one does not, of what use is he to us?

‡ There is a necessary distinction between what God is in himself and what he is for us. We are aware of the same distinction whenever we look at a beautiful landscape. We only feel its beauty when we see it in a particular light and from a particular distance and angle. When we get close enough to it, it ceases to be a landscape at all.

‡ 'Homo sapiens, the only creature endowed with reason, is the only one to pin its existence to irrational things. There must surely be some good reason for this' (Bergson). The explanation of course is that men do not live by reason, but are merely controlled by it. Otherwise why do they fall in love and practise the arts?

‡ The lottery theory of life. Without losses, there cannot be gains, without risks there cannot be triumphs. So, if the roulette board is

honestly designed, this is the best of all worlds and every evil in it is a necessary evil. That is to say, if we want life we must accept the conditions that are necessary for life, for Utopia is not life. Thus, though men should aspire to justice in their social organization, since justice is the law of social animals, they should not expect justice from God because justice is inconsistent with his gift of life. In fact, as Dante says in *Canto* VII of the *Inferno*, he has appointed Fortune, who is one of the primal Creatures or Sub-Deities, to run the lottery we need, but often complain of, for ourselves. There is therefore no 'problem of evil'.

This would seem to be a plausible explanation of the world as we experience it, yet when we are faced with calamities such as the death of Keats or of one of our children, how smug it seems!

‡ Yet if many of the calamities in our lives come from what we call natural causes, by far the worst and most numerous come from our own evil actions. We can hardly blame God for this, for if we had not been given a choice between good and evil we could not claim to be responsible creatures. It is the fact that we are more intelligent and inventive than the animals that allows us that enormous scope for cruelty and evil which the history of the present century illustrates so well. The animals kill for food and do not see beyond that: we prey on our own kind.

‡ Socrates thought that wickedness came from ignorance. We know better now. Just as goodness comes from a good disposition, so wickedness comes from an evil one. We carry our dispositions in our genes, and circumstance and opportunity bring them out.

‡ 'I do not believe in God because if he existed he would long ago have destroyed the human race for its cruelty and evil.' Whoever said this was perhaps not far off the mark.

‡ In every class and age, of every race and persuasion, there are good and bad people. What a pity that we cannot form a closed society of the good, banishing to another planet the violent, the fanatical, the power-greedy, the unjust, the mercenary, the cruel!

The Prophet Isaiah believed that on 'the Lord's Day', as he called it, God would annihilate the bad and spare the good – whom, being a pessimist, he spoke of as 'a small remnant'. How is it then that God has never thought fit to take up this excellent idea? A deadly virus that would attack only the bad would be well within his creative capacity and is just what is needed to make the world habitable. We cannot perform this operation for ourselves without joining the ranks of those we are destroying, so we need to have it done for us. This is just one of those things that since Biblical times we have kept a God for.

‡ *Ilusión*. This Spanish word does not mean 'illusion', or something that is false, but the natural hopes and expectations that maintain people during their lives. For, from the strictly Catholic point of view, these are false too. This ambiguity gives the word a certain melancholy.

‡ I lay awake last night evolving a heresy. It is that God does not care for the individual, but only for the species. It is Christ who cares for the individual. He came down to rescue him and to reconcile him to God. But now the Marxists are attempting to undo the work of Christ and to restore the Old Law.

‡ Only the unhappy want a future life. The rest of us would like a longer spell in this one; yet, because we feel this, how much grandeur has gone out of the world, how human nature has contracted! Our race has lost its old colonies in the skies and in the depths and so it feels weaker and less important.

‡ If it were not for death there would be no urgency about religion. It would be all praise and poetry and the celebration of life. However since we do not know what life is, nor what time is, nor what anything is – because, as the scientists have found, everything turns into something else the moment we examine it – I take it we do not know about death either. Our fear of it is like that of children who are frightened of the dark. But I trust life and the values we discover in life, which for the sake of the attitudes

generated by that word I am willing to call God. Having found them to be good, should I not therefore trust the whole process?

‡ Belief in a future life is a great inducement to religious faith, but a barrier to honest religion because it shows that the greed and self-interest that a religious faith ought to destroy has merely been postponed to another existence. Thus the moral value of a religion can be tested by what it says about death.

‡ 'The Gauls, taught by the Druids, are so firmly convinced that their souls are immortal that they are said to lend one another sums of money to be repaid in the next world. I would call this foolish indeed if it was not that what these trousered barbarians believe is the very faith of the Greek Pythagoras himself' (Valerius Maximus, early first century A.D.).

‡ *On Mu Tsung* (821–824). 'And Mu Tsung died from an over-dose of the medicine of immortality' (quoted in an article by Peter Russell).

‡ What we see today is perhaps not so much the decline of Christianity as that of the last vestiges of paganism with its rites and customs, which once embraced the whole of life from the cradle to the grave. The Church adopted these, throwing over them its own colours. Now where are we? In an entirely lay world which, as the Communists and Nazis have shown, provides no sanctions for the old morality.

‡ If it is true, as I believe it to be, that St Paul brought about the change of Christianity from a Jewish Messiah cult to a Greek mystery religion concerned with personal salvation and survival after death, how is it that the Catholic Church does not hold the Eleusinian Mysteries, the rites of the Orphics and of Adonis and Attis, in the same esteem as the Old Testament? For if the Jewish national religion gave the stock, the Greek gardener's richer cutting was grafted onto it.

‡ Christian piety is Jewish, but its myths and festivals are Greek and pagan.

‡ Christianity is not a philosophic religion like Buddhism or Neo-platonism, but, like Judaism, a historical one. It explains history as a gradual unfolding, beginning slowly and coming to a crisis. Its culmination, the Crucifixion, happened only once. It is thus not easily susceptible to Platonic treatment, and had not a religious and philosophic genius like St Augustine come along it would never have acquired this.

‡ There are two branches of Christianity: that which derives from the teaching and personality of Jesus as revealed in the Gospels, and that given us by St Paul, according to which the Crucifixion and Ascension were supernatural events which make a complete break in the history of man by redeeming him from sin and death. By the end of the first century these two had coalesced, but today they are separating again. There is no credibility problem about the first.

‡ One of the problems of every institutional religion comes from the tendency of ordinary people to turn what are properly myths or allegories into concrete facts. Every Church has to face this: how can the language of religious thought and feeling be made to cater both for subtle and for simple minds?

‡ Atheists who feel a hatred of religion usually do so because they have received it at its crudest and most anthropomorphic. In the same way a person who has only heard the light music that is played in parks might suppose that this was the only music.

‡ There are two sorts of atheist – those who merely say that they do not believe in God and those who assert that he does not and cannot exist, and that it is superstitious and contrary to reason to believe that he does. The second class, the dogmatic atheists, are simply Victorian clergymen stood on their heads – that is to say,

people who are certain and positive that they understand the scheme of things.

‡ Most citizens of the United States, if they wish to be regarded as decent and respectable persons, must belong to some religion, whether Catholic, Episcopalian, Mormon, Jewish, Christian Scientist or Seventh-day Adventist. It does not matter which.

‡ 'Religion is a defensive reaction of Nature to the dissolvent power of the intelligence' (Bergson). For when the tribe begins to expand and its bonds to weaken, men tend to forget that they are social creatures and, incited by their intelligence, live for self-interest. Religion then becomes the guardian of society, its power increasing in lawless and chaotic ages and declining in orderly and prosperous ones.

‡ An atheism founded on rational or philosophic grounds, as Bertrand Russell once said to me, is not tenable because there can be no proof that God does not exist. But an atheism founded on moral grounds has more to be said for it, for, if God is omnipotent, how can he allow such enormous suffering to exist in the world? Jesus had believed that a great moral change – the establishment of the Kingdom of God – was about to come in, which would at one stroke abolish all evil and suffering, but this has not happened. Theology came into existence to find a way round the problem.

‡ The greatest enemies of religion have always been the religious people themselves, more particularly the *dévots*, who got an egotistical satisfaction from displaying their beliefs and trying to dominate other people with them. Today they have lost their power, but the harm has been done. The Victorian bishops and clergymen are the real fathers of atheism in England.

‡ 'There is no malignity so great as the Christian. Our zeal does wonders when it eggs on our bent for hatred, cruelty, ambition,

avarice, calumny or rebellion. On the other hand, whenever it is a question of goodness, kind-heartedness or moderation, unless by miracle some rare inclination says it, it goes neither by foot nor on wings' (Montaigne, *Essays*).

‡ The paradox of Christianity. Jesus said, 'Love your enemies.' Yet the religion that is practised in his name has been for much of the time a school for hatred. No other religion, neither Buddhism nor Hinduism nor Islam, has shown such malignity and cruelty, as, among other things, the history of the persecution of the Jews reveals. Yet Christianity drew its fanaticism from its Jewish root, as a reading of the Old Testament will tell one.

‡ 'In the nineteenth century the average length of life for clergy-men was eighty-one years, for politicians seventy-seven years and for atheists and sceptics sixty-four years' (David Ogg, *Europe of the Ancien Régime*). So it paid then to believe in God.

‡ One of the principal reasons for the decline of Christianity today has been its stern attitude to sex. This does not stem so much from its early phase of extreme asceticism, for that has long ceased to exist, as from its having inherited the cold sexual pattern of the Mediterranean countries, which was founded on the chastity of women and their role in society as bearers of children to their husbands. In the religious revival that took place in Victorian England sexual conduct became almost the sole touchstone of morality, so that when the rebellion against that broke out early in this century and was followed by a glorification of sex, the young deserted the churches. Today we look back with repulsion on the Church's attitude to sex as well as on its indifference to cruelty and torture, but the founder of Christianity cannot be blamed for these.

‡ Comparing Santayana to William James, Bertrand Russell remarks on the temperamental opposition persisting between Catholic and Protestant free-thinkers. Of course. There is so much more in religion than faith. There is a life-style.

‡ According to Sun Yat Sen one of the most striking characteristics of European civilization is the inconsistency between its words and its deeds. Thus, though Europe was the richest and most acquisitive region of the world, it had a religion which idealized poverty. This had led to a state of hypocrisy and double thinking which was incomprehensible to simple Orientals. Yet was this such a bad thing? One might argue that the tension which Christianity set up between men's ideals and their natural desires has been one of the most productive and energy-giving things in Western civilization. It gave men guilt.

‡ A way of putting things. Jesus overcame the law of gravity, which is a symbol of the original sin that weighs men down to earth. Thus he was able to walk on the water, lift diseases off men's shoulders and ascend into the air. But he never overcame the Second Law of Thermodynamics, or entropy, and so he failed. In human terms this is the dullness and hebetude in which we spend the greater part of our lives and which ends by whittling away all feelings and enthusiasm.

‡ Jesus, the spirit of penetrating ideas, of disconcerting acts and words, of wit and poetry.

‡ According to Nietzsche, paganism is the religion that says yes to all that is natural, whereas Christianity says no to it. But he holds that Jesus was not responsible for this. In *The Will to Power* he asserts that the doctrine of Jesus is as pure and wholesome as that of Zarathustra. Saying yes to life sounds pleasant and human, yet perhaps saying no to it leads to a greater dynamism because it sets up a neurosis.

‡ Christianity flourishes in proportion to the misery and insecurity of life. Prosperity kills it because at its most sincere it is a cry from the depths. It is declining today in the Western world because of the great rise in the standard of living, but if this were to be interrupted or to prove unsatisfying it would revive again, though in other forms.

‡ The social function of religion is to satisfy anxiety. A man who believes in God has a secret aid he can call on. An illusion? Let him who has no illusions be the first to find fault.

‡ We live between two ages. The old religion is dying and the new one, which we must have if we are to grow to our full height, has not yet been born. So we waver, and either take up art as a compromise or keep to a material plane.

‡ We need not always consider Christianity as a matter of personal faith. It is also the guardian of our rites and ceremonies, of our traditional modes of feeling and thinking. The outward and visible forms of our culture are bound up with it. It thus seems perfectly natural and proper that people who do not believe in it should be married and buried with religious ceremonies.

‡ Catholicism is the fulfilment of paganism, so paganism is dying too. Instead of Midsummer Eve we now have Bank Holiday.

‡ Today the dry rot is working in every timber of our *domus*. The religious timbers are the first to go, but others are threatened. What remains is the cult of science, the most abstract of all our undertakings, which only very few people can understand. This is because it produces useful results, such as the telephone, the aeroplane and television, but has it increased our zest for life or even our safety?

‡ Today we members of the cultured élite are all polytheists. The gods we worship are Mozart and Beethoven, Titian and Cézanne, Shakespeare and Baudelaire, while some of us shown an even greater devotion to our local deities, the spirits of the woods and streams. Enlighten me, D. H. Lawrence; comfort me, Ivy Compton Burnett; make me yours, Ezra Pound! The young too have their special *numina*, the crooners and pop singers, more intense if less enduring, to match ours.

‡ The ancient Greeks believed that the gods drew their strength from the sacrifices made to them by men. If these ceased they would, though immortal, lose all their power. So, according to some Protestant theologians, the Christian God has died because men have ceased to believe in him. This is to suppose that God is in a certain sense dependent on men. Yet not entirely, because he may, if he ever existed, have merely withdrawn from the human scene.

‡ In my flirtations with religion I have always regarded it as something designed to bless life. For that reason it has never made a strong impact on me. But true religion, the religion that people ask for and get, exists to assure them that there is a meaning and purpose in life as well as a road to be followed which accords with these. Since I have always believed in my bones that life had a meaning and that I had a path marked out for me, I have never taken it very personally. I merely try to understand it and in this shallow and reductionist age to stand up for the rights of other people to believe in it.

‡ I cannot be a humanist because I do not feel that Man is a sufficiently noble animal to be given absolute power over his destiny. Then I am conscious of belonging not only to the human race, but to the whole body of living creatures. The hare and the olive tree are my brothers, the lion and the toad. For that reason I need some authority that is higher than human law to look up to. What authority I do not know, but my need has made me a fellow traveller of the religious, though I shall get out of their bus several stations before the end.

‡ The voice of God is no doubt a reflection of our own voice from the stratosphere, but it returns to us with more authority than it left us. Is this because our conscience, whose voice it is, has become more refined and purified on its passage?

‡ The *enaciados* were those Spaniards of the early Middle Ages who belonged either to both or to neither religion, the Christian

3   BTT

and the Moslem, and betrayed each in turn to the other. They lived
on the frontier and sometimes made up whole villages, for instance
the Puebla de Naciados in Estremadura. It would seem that I am
one of them, placed between Christianity and agnosticism, and
with a foot in both camps. But I see no need to choose.

‡ Impurity, indicating a state of being, is a Greek conception.
Sin, meaning an offence against God – that is a deed – is mainly
a Jewish one. Without their discovery of the importance of sin
there would be no Jews in the world today, for it was by means
of it that they absolved their tribal god Jahweh from his habit of
continually letting them down and took the blame for their mis-
fortunes on their own shoulders. This secured their continuity, for
if in those days a God lost face by letting his people be defeated,
they broke up – trust in him being the only thing that held them
together. So they repented and started again. In the Christian age
sin has been an immensely productive notion, strengthening and
consolidating the ego in its trials and giving a transcendental
importance to the petty incidents of life.

‡ 'The Iroquois have properly speaking only one divinity, which
is the dream' (a Jesuit missionary to the Hurons in 1670). This is
a very individualist religion since it makes every man his own
priest.

‡ 'Catholicism is the most human of religions if taken seriously;
it is paganism spiritually transformed and made metaphysical. It
corresponds most adequately to the various exigencies of moral
life, with just the needed dose of wisdom, sublimity and illusion.
Only it should be accepted humanly, traditionally as part of an
unquestioned order, a moral heritage, like one's language and
family life, leaving religious controversy to the synods and metaphysical speculation to the schools' (Santayana, *Persons and
Places*).

‡ 'Liberalism, Protestantism, Judaism, positivism all have the
same ultimate aim and standard. It is prosperity or, as Lutheran

theologians put it, union with God on our level, not at God's
level. The thing all these schools detest is the idea of union with
God at God's level, proper to asceticism, mysticism, Platonism
and pure intelligence, which insist on seeing things under the form
of Truth and Eternity. You must be content, they say, to see things
under the form of Time, of appearance and of feeling' (Santayana,
Persons and Places).

I am a liberal and was brought up as an Anglican, but I admire
the Catholic view because it is more demanding. It is by attempting
the impossible that one goes furthest.

‡ 'Now as I was come up in spirit through the Flaming Sword
into the Paradise of God, all things were new, and all creation
gave another smell to me than before, beyond what words can
utter. I knew nothing but pureness, and innocency and righteous-
ness, being received into the image of God by Jesus Christ, so
that I can say that I was come up to the state of Adam, which
he was in before he fell. The Creation was opened unto me'
(George Fox, *Journals*).

‡ Miracles are like jokes. They relieve our tension suddenly by
setting us free from the chain of cause and effect.

‡ St Rumwold of Kings Sutton, Northants, was born around the
year 630 and died three days later. These days he spent preaching
to his parents on the pomps and vanities of life.

‡ The Blessed Giovanni Giuseppe della Croce, who died in 1634,
possessed the rare gift of bilocation – that is of being in two
places at the same time. Numerous examples of his having done
this are given in the proceedings for his beatification in 1789,
which were undertaken as a confutation of the incredulity and
mockery of Voltaire.

‡ The Blessed Giovanni de Copertino (1630–1663) could not pray
without being carried up into the air. He flew around churches,

whirling above the heads of the congregation, sometimes carrying one of them with him, and whenever there was a procession he would follow it down the street ten feet above the heads of the people, although, to avoid causing a sensation, he tried his hardest to keep on the ground. The Church authorities disapproved of these unedifying exhibitions and confined him to his priory, but not before immense numbers of people, including cardinals, had witnessed his flights. Since there is a great deal more evidence for the Blessed Giovanni's aerial exploits than there is for the victory of William the Conqueror at the battle of Hastings, one may ask why the religious authorities were so anxious to hush them up.

‡ There is a certain whimsical humour about some of the relics preserved in churches. The eminent Spanish humanist Alfonso de Valdés (1490–1552) describes those he saw in a convent church near Rome. In addition to the usual drops of Virgin's milk and feathers pulled from the tail of the Holy Ghost and nails from the Holy Cross there was a bottle containing the breath of the donkey that had stood in the stable at Bethlehem when Jesus was born.

‡ 'If Cardinal Jacques de Vitry is to be believed, the nuns of Liège in the thirteenth century were much given to mystic raptures; of one of them he relates that she often had twenty-five raptures a day, while others passed years in bed, dissolved in floods of divine love' (Lea, *History of the Inquisition*, vol. IV).

‡ There are two St Anthonys who are highly regarded in Spain. One is the hermit of the Egyptian desert who lived in the second century and is today associated with pigs, and the other is St Anthony of Padua, a Franciscan friar who finds things when they have been lost. Once not long ago a builder who was a devout adherent of the second saint was working on a high block of flats. He slipped and overbalanced and as he fell through the air he cried out, 'Saint Anthony, save me!' A terrible voice was heard demanding, 'Which Saint Anthony?' 'That of Padua,' the man replied. Crash. He had named the wrong one.

‡ Should there be a summing up?...The religious instinct has existed in man for the past million years and has passed through many different forms and stages. Its essence among civilized people today can be described as an aspiration towards a morally and spiritually better life. Historically – that is during the past three or four millennia – it has been associated with the word God and much of this aura still clings to it and gives it a stronger psychological impact. Embodied in an all-powerful and transcendent person or poured into a metaphysical concept, it has a pull that it could not easily have otherwise, for it is by this means that it acquires a form, a body, a coherence that are necessary if it is to have a deep root in the psyche or be shared with others and given a social role and function. Without this root, without this more or less anthropomorphic projection, it would lack driving force and remain a mere vague and ill-defined private ideal. It is for this reason that it is apt to contain irrational elements, the products of faith or vision, though not necessarily any that contradict the picture of the world given us by science.

But how, it may be asked, does this religious aspiration differ from other aspirations, for example the political and humanitarian ones, which are equally idealistic? The answer is that it comes from the depths of a man's being, is involved with his personal struggles and dilemmas and covers the whole field of his life. It can thus enrich and deepen the personality and, since a strong religious conviction is often the result of private troubles and calamities, it can give consolation. Not everyone has the religious temperament, just as not everyone has an artistic or a psychologically intuitive one, but they are not so far apart as is often supposed.

Art & architecture

‡ Art organizes the visual world for the emotions as science does for the intellect.

‡ In the history of culture works of art and literature occupy the place of beneficial mutations in biology, offering new possibilities of feeling and awareness for man.

‡ What is art? Language? Art can be said to speak a language since its function is to communicate, but essentially a work of art is a sort of dynamo that gives out energy. When we are properly adjusted to receive its radiations we find ourselves raised to a new and higher state of being that leaves us enriched and satisfied. In its early stages it was a fetish, something that aroused supernatural feelings even in its maker, and it still keeps today some of its original magical quality.

‡ 'O blessed rage for order, pale Ramon!' The kind of order required for art is different from that required for science and philosophy and appeals to different parts of the mind, but both fulfil a deep human need. For in art order is the same thing as meaning.

‡ Art teaches us to see as men saw before they invented language, for as soon as we have a word for a thing we cease to see it as it is and take in no more of it than we need in order to recognize it and record it in our catalogue. Thus art helps to liberate us from

what is automatic and mechanical in our lives and restores to us that pure, untarnished vision that makes the joy of small children and of animals.

‡ Works of art and literature are not an entertainment or a diversion to amuse our leisure, but the one serious and enduring achievement of mankind – the notches on the bank of an irrigation channel which record the height to which the water once rose. If few people have a sense for them, that is their loss, for they are always there waiting to be felt and experienced. All they demand is receptivity, which is another way of saying openness to life, though on a different plane. It is from this difference of plane, which heightens and clarifies, that the value of art derives.

‡ 'Science can never reach its final goal, whereas art is always at its goal' (Schopenhauer).

‡ 'First we look at the hills in the painting, then we look at the painting in the hills' (Li Liweng, 17th century). It is in this way that nature imitates art.

‡ The distinguishing mark of a good painting is not its beauty or its correspondence to reality, but its vitality. That is, a vitality caused by the inner tensions of its various parts and held together in a state of equilibrium that makes it one complete and self-enclosed thing. The value of a sketch or drawing lies in its power of suggestion.

‡ Painters require an idea to work by, even more than poets or novelists do. The history of painting since Giotto has been largely the history of these ideas. Yet they should not stand out in their work. Many of Paolo Uccello's frescoes suffer because he was too obsessed by his search for correct perspective, whereas Masaccio mastered the whole matter intuitively. Similarly only art critics or historians need to be aware of the scientific theories of light that underlie Impressionism or of the ideas on the construction of space

that went to the making of Cubism. No doubt it is interesting to read analyses of paintings and so enter more deeply into what the painter was aiming at and doing, but the essential thing is to look at them and submit to the feeling they give us. The eye of the viewer must be innocent and free from theories. These can come later to stimulate the sluggishness of our responses and direct our minds to what we have failed to take in.

‡ 'Je fais profession des choses muettes...Traiter la Nature non comme un modèle a interpréter, mais comme un langage par lequel s'exprimeront et se communiqueront les diverses émotions humaines.' 'My concern is with dumb things...I treat Nature not as a model to be interpreted, but as a language through which the various human emotions find expression and communicate themselves' (Poussin).

‡ 'Everyone wants to understand painting. Why don't they try to understand the singing of birds? People love the night, a flower, everything that surrounds them without trying to understand them. But painting – that they *must* understand' (Picasso).

‡ 'Negro sculpture is a mediator between the sculptor and the hostile powers surrounding him, in order to overcome his fear and horror by giving it a form and an image...This is what all art is about. It isn't an aesthetic operation; it's a form of magic designed to mediate between this strange hostile world and ourselves, a way of seizing power by giving form to our terrors as well as to our desires. When I came to realize this, I knew that I had found my way' (Picasso).

Goya might have said the same thing.

‡ Every large picture gallery is the scene of a struggle to the death between certain of the paintings. There they are, the world-famous beauty queens, doing their best to hook the innocents who pass in front of them and to draw their attention away from the other paintings to themselves. Titians lord it over Grecos, Piero della Francescas turn a cold stare on Rubenses, Goyas jeer

at Raphaels. Feelings run high and the dazed visitor, like Paris trying to decide to which of the goddesses he should give his apple, has to hurry off to the bar to restore his equanimity.

‡ In more select galleries pictures stand back and watch the passers-by. Like Victorian ladies in a street they bow only to those who recognize them.

‡ Italian art of the high Renaissance is aristocratic and ecclesiastical and its subjects are therefore idealized in accordance with the Platonic tendencies of the age. But Dutch art is middle-class and plebeian and requires actuality and particularity. Thus Vermeer's women are real women sitting in real rooms, and if they often transport us by their beauty we put this down to the effect of the slanting light falling on rich interiors and not to any general theory of sublimation.

‡ It is remarkable how many painters of the classical Renaissance, whose usual productions consist of large canvases painted in an idealized or generalized manner, have left portraits that show considerable psychological penetration. Raphael is the most pre-eminent of these, but among the secondary painters it is often the portraits that one most wants to look at. Then it would seem that complexity of character in the sitter will often bring out an extra sensitivity in the painter, as may be seen in Holbein's portrait of Erasmus or in Antonio Mor's of Queen Mary Tudor (in the Prado), where the whole of her sad and thwarted history can be read in her features. Just as a good doctor can often diagnose the beginnings of illness in a face, so the painter's eye can read deep into the state of consciousness of his sitter. So what are we to say of Francis Bacon?

‡ Some paintings yield their full effect instantaneously while others give it out by slow degrees. One example of the first is Botticelli's *Birth of Venus*. On seeing it for the first time I was struck with amazement at its beauty and freshness and said to myself that it was the greatest picture ever painted, the herald of a new Spring-

time when all the flowers of poetry and culture were about to burst into blossom. But it made a weaker impression when I looked at it again a few years later, for in spite of its flowing, musical line and the perfection of the whole composition, the image it left in the mind was too simplified. The greatest art is always complex and hugs some of its secrets to itself, whereas one could almost say that there is something of the stereotype behind this too perfect work. One turns then to the *Primavera*, whose composition is more complex, if not a little confused.

Poussin is one of the many examples of a painter the full force of whose pictures comes through more slowly because their learned and intellectual construction is not so immediately revealed. Every time I see one of his paintings, faded and grimed though its colours may be, I discover more in it. Yet Michelangelo, that superman among artists, overwhelms one immediately and there is never any going back on that first impression.

‡ The pictures that move me most are those that express a moment in time when things seem to have been arrested and made to stand still. Nothing in them can change, nothing be altered, for eternity has set its stamp on them. Among modern painters Cézanne and the earlier Seurat give me this feeling as Piero della Francesca and Giovanni Bellini do among the ancients – also in a rather different way some of Perugino's figures, standing immobile on a hilltop beside their spindly trees with the wide spaces of air spreading round them. For this reason I am not drawn to Rubens because in his paintings every little detail is on the move. Nothing has weight, there is no rest for the mind, one thinks chiefly of the skill and mastery. But also of the exuberant feeling for life.

‡ It is possible for a not very good picture to suggest far more than it actually gives. Thus the frescoes in the Villa dei Misteri at Pompeii convince us that the Greeks had a school of painting that, as they claimed, was equal in greatness to their literature. The mosaic of the Battle of Issus between Alexander and Darius, which is said to be a reproduction of a late Alexandrian painting, confirms this, for only a great tradition could produce such a masterly composition.

‡ Italian painting of the Renaissance aims at giving reassurance, which it does by showing that the world is beautiful and harmonious. French painting, though with an increasing adherence to the truth of visual appearances, has on the whole followed the same road. But Spanish painting, as we see it in Goya, Picasso and Miró, is sharply disruptive and delights in exposing the cruelty and rottenness that lie beneath the imposing façade. Even in Velazquez there is often something disquieting. He is a painter who is so much in love with light impinging on smooth surfaces that he allows it to destroy or over-rule the human values which, as we can see from the subjects he chose to paint, he genuinely cared for in his aloof and detached way. His kings and princesses are dolls and his great portrait of Pope Innocent III at Rome has a sinister quality that makes one understand its attraction for Francis Bacon.

‡ It is not the large art galleries that attract me most with their jostle of tourists and schoolchildren, but the small provincial ones, or else those churches where there is perhaps only a single picture to be seen. Take for example Castelfranco with its huge moated castle and its diminutive Giorgione, which I first saw in 1912 hanging in a deserted chapel, but which has since been transferred to a small cell-like structure into which one peers through an iron grille. Then there is Borgo San Sepolcro. I well remember my first visit to it with my wife over forty years ago. Piero della Francesca's *Resurrection* hung alone in a small room, and it seemed to me then and still seems to me today the most powerful and expressive painting in the world.

In the early light of dawn the risen Christ breaks with such force and majesty from his tomb that the sleeping soldiers have been driven back against the earth by the recoil from his ascent. On his face there still lies all the sadness and solemnity of the grave, while his powerful upsurge displays his triumphant conquest over it. As a friend of mine, an ardent hater of religion, once said to me, 'If anything could convert me to Christianity it would be that picture.' We came away and as we passed the market place I saw a dead wolf that had just been shot in the vicinity hanging from a pole.

‡ In sightseeing the amateur who knows little of art history has always the exciting possibility of discovering something that will move him deeply, but which he had not heard of before. Only two years ago I had just such an experience in the church of San Clemente in Rome. I had visited it several times before, but on each occasion had overlooked the chapel of Saint Catherine with its frescoes by Masolino da Panicale, because until the electric light is turned on it is nothing but a dark cave. Now Masolino is not one of the major painters and none of the work I had seen of his had impressed me much. In Florence he is overshadowed by his pupil Masaccio. But as soon as the light came on in the little chapel his frescoes carried me away. The decoration of the whole interior formed a perfect unity: the scenes on the side walls were very delicately painted while the central Crucifixion, seen above the bars of a *reja*, made a tremendous impact. Sublimity is the only word to use and I came away with the sense of having had a religious experience that united me in feeling to the men of that century.

‡ In certain moods a visit to an art gallery can leave one with a feeling of deep sadness. All these beautiful young women and handsome men staring out from their frames were once alive, but are now dead. One calls up Villon's poem – 'où sont les neiges d'antan?' – There they sit, those venerable figures of the past, high on their Parnassus, keeping an anxious eye on the work of their descendants. The painters of our time whom the great Venetians admire most are Matisse and Bonnard, whereas Piero della Francesca only thinks well of Cézanne and Seurat. Leonardo confesses to a slight weakness for Pollock, and Bosch is strongly hooked on Klee and Miró. But what they are most concerned about is to know whether they themselves are still looked up to and admired as they were in their own day. How are the sales going? Are sacrifices still offered to them?

‡ The past fifty years have seen not so much a revolution in art as an explosion. After the discovery of primitive African wood carvings had opened a breach, the main movement lay through the synthetic style of Cubism, but since then Surrealism has been a

great and disruptive influence. This began in 1920 as a wildly romantic and anti-rational movement initiated by enthusiastic young writers who had been inspired by the discoveries of Freud concerning the unconscious, and though it has led to some of the worst painting that any art movement has ever produced, it also gave a permissiveness to the imagination that has affected, sometimes beneficially, the whole art world.

Meanwhile painting in Germany had taken with Paul Klee an even more revolutionary turn, for he set out to give a graphic form to ideas and non-visual sensations and to offer comments on them of a lyrical or humorous kind. This opened up an entirely new field for art, while in Paris Joan Miró, a Catalan who had started as a surrealist, began to paint in an obscure style of signs or symbols, sometimes influenced by Picasso, with the aim, as he said, of 'reaching a goal beyond painting'. In some inexplicable way his hieroglyphs often worked.

But by this time a total anarchy had descended upon the world of art which can be compared to the anarchy that round 1970 affected the dress style of the hippies. The artist ceased to be a person who painted scenes or objects in a way that derived, however remotely, from the past, and launched out into the jungle of his own fantasies. Many of these productions, especially those in which the inspiration was mainly literary, took the form of gestures or manifestos expressing the views of some little art group and whose only object seemed to be to shock or surprise. Symbols too, following the fashion set for them by Jung, began to proliferate, though no one knew what they symbolized. No doubt, as Turner remarked, 'art is a rum go', but this seemed like individual caprice run mad.

What future art historians will think of this period is a matter for speculation. Will they regard it as a sign of the final decadence and imminent breakdown of European capitalism, with its loss of a sense of social responsibility and its iconoclastic fragmentation, or as an adventurous era of experiment to enlarge the frontiers of art which can be compared either to the investigations of the depth psychologists or to the work of the physicists in splitting the atom? At all events, some time in the forties or fifties this phase of art began to pass out and a reaction began which led to a return to pure painting without any representational or psychological overtones. That is, to the austere style of abstraction.

‡ Picasso's death ends an epoch. His career has been more like that of a lyric or satiric poet than that of a painter, for after he emerged from his Cubist period he set himself no fixed objective or programme in his painting, showed no desire for continuity or development, but lashed out in any direction that suited his mood of the moment. His consciousness of his enormous talent allowed him to do this without any pause in his energy, but his work took on a more and more critical and satirical tone, from his pastiches of the work of other art periods to his brilliant drawings of the model, the painter and the monkey. Except when he was under the influence of his feelings about the Spanish Civil War, when he painted *Guernica*, he made little attempt to produce great pictures, but threw off one rapidly executed canvas after another. Thus, though more gifted than almost any painter or draughtsman has ever been, his intensely personal and destructive attitude makes him a disconcerting figure, a sort of Mephistopheles of art, lacking any integration with his own age, though unfortunately very influential in it. John Berger's study of him is one of the best pieces of art criticism of our time.

‡ *Abstract painting.* This is an art form which often has the power to please and satisfy, but which does not seem likely ever to give rise to great masterpieces. One reason for this is that it leaves too much liberty to the artist. In representational art the need to paint a picture that will conform to some of the facts of visual appearances imposes a discipline as well as giving a point of departure. Take the case of a portrait. Through the features of the sitter's perhaps insignificant face the artist must drive the deep feeling that its form arouses in him, so that, while keeping the likeness, it becomes something much more than this man's face. Of course painters differ in their approach to the model. For some, such as Cézanne, the grasping of the formal properties of a face or head will be the main object and the likeness will appear as if by accident: for others, such as Rubens or Goya, the character and life revealed in the sitter's features will be the thing to be seized, but in both cases the painter's deep instinctive feeling will have been both stimulated and controlled by the subject he is painting. In this way there is set up in his mind and hand a complicated reverberation between the model he sees before him and the canvas, and with it that heightened feeling that nervous tension always gives. Then from the viewer's point of view the fact that

this is both a human face and also something much more significant
– an entity in the super-real world of art – is important. All the
mixed feelings and experiences that human life provides are brought
in and focussed upon this picture. Rembrandt's *Margarita van
Tripp* is the exact likeness of an old lady, but also how much
more! And it could not be that much more unless it was an exact
likeness. It is the same with figure paintings and landscapes. Just
as the artist's mind has been stimulated by the scenes of real life
which will later pour out of him with heightened intensity onto
his canvas, so the viewer is stimulated by the references he gets to
things that he can recognize, and this enhances and illuminates the
feeling that the picture gives him. The art of the past has a rich
content both in humanity and in Nature and something is inevitably
lost when the link between them is broken.

Now abstract art is the product of men living in large, featureless
cities, cut off from the stir and bustle of human life because there
is no drama in the streets, which are just drains in which people
hurry blindly along, and cut off too from easy contact with
Nature. It is not because, as is often said, photography gives a
more exact likeness of people and places, since exact likeness has
never been one of the aims of art, that many of our painters and
sculptors have deserted the world of visual experience, but because
like fish in underground streams they have lost their power to get
stimulus from it. So they retreat into their studio-laboratories and
draw their paintings out of their own ideas and ruminations. This
means that there is no struggle in their canvases, no tension – only
choices and hesitations. And of course no reference to human
life or Nature, except when sometimes they have come to abstract
painting after a long practice of figurative art and their forms are
drawn out of their feelings for natural objects. Yet abstract paintings
can give great rewards, often more immediately than figurative
ones. That is because they appeal solely to the aesthetic sense,
delighting the eye by their delicate forms and textures and contrasts
of tone. Our natural taste for geometric forms as a rest from
organic ones can be stimulated or, as in the case of the Tachists, the
pleasure that we get from looking at the markings on old walls
or palings or on the barks of trees. This sort of painting demands
of the abstract painter the finest sensibility and often much invention, though he will inevitably lack what Francis Bacon gives
us – 'the fury and the mire of human veins'. One can also say of
abstract paintings that they are often more easily acclimatized on

the walls of private houses than are representational paintings
because, being nearer in kind to decoration, they do not demand
so insistently to be closely looked at, but form points of rest for
the eye in a room. (P.S. To avoid confusion I should add that
I have used the term 'abstract art' to describe any painting which
is not concerned with representing objects in nature, whether it is
geometrical like a Mondrian, or organic like a Gorky, or resembles
those of Pollock or Rothko. Painters use various terms.)

‡ Is it true, as some people claim, that abstract art is more closely
related to music than is figurative art because it has freed itself
from all association with actual things? In theory this may be so,
but the resemblance does not appear in practice. Speaking generally,
it is not easy to see much correspondence between painting and
music, because the one exists in space and the other in time or, as
Bergson would put it, in duration. If there is any, one would
expect to find it in paintings which express linear movement, and
in fact Lord Clark does find it in Botticelli's vital, flowing line,
while others have seen in paintings by Giorgione or Watteau an
emotional equivalent to a Mozart sonata. But where does one find
in abstract painting or sculpture a work which suggests such a
comparison? The feature that music and painting share is rhythm
and is less evident in abstract art than in any other. Nor is there
ever an equivalent in mood.

However one must remember that abstraction in painting is not
as new or as unique as its contemporary practitioners suppose. The
difference between a photograph and even the most realistic
painting – say, one of Courbet's landscapes – is that in the latter
there has been selection, emphasis and some discreet distortion.
The painter's deep instinctive feeling for mass and force has re-
arranged everything. It is only after we have seen a Courbet
landscape that we get a sense of the weight and pressure of a
mountain slope or the force of a breaking wave. Before that we
were hardly aware of them when we met with them in Nature, and
yet these are abstract ideas. Now much of the art of the Italian
Renaissance from Raphael to Giorgione and again in Poussin
depends on its property of abstraction from reality. Their subjects
are highly generalized, treated like the poetry of that age in an
ideal or sublimated manner, for the reason that any touch of realism
would produce a clash or interruption in the harmony of the

design. The flow of the rhythm through the picture is the first requirement, the active and harmonious relation of all its parts, while the subject, after working for the Church ceased to be necessary, is a mythological dreamland which is in harmony with the general style and execution. Raphael, that great master of pictorial composition, is a prime example of this. Although no one could paint a more vivid or psychologically penetrating portrait than he, the faces in his great compositions are conventional or even insipid because the general design of the picture required it. This has prejudiced many people today against him, but in acting in this way he was following his general principle of abstraction or generalization for the sake of the picture as a whole. Does this art of painting have any affinity with music? One can only say that Michelangelo thought so, as may be seen from a quotation from one of his letters: 'Good painting', he wrote, 'is a music and a melody which only the intellect can appreciate, and that with great difficulty. This kind of painting is so rare that few are capable of doing it or attaining to it.'

‡ *Abstract expressionism.* This is the name adopted by a group of some thirty painters who first got together in New York in 1947 and have since made that city the capital of the art world. Most of them had come out of Surrealism with its sexual or mythological symbolism and its theory of reliance on accident, but though a few of them, such as Arshile Gorky, retained a link with this, the others made a complete break, which sometimes took the form of a sudden conversion. The chief novelty was that the painter no longer approached his canvas with an idea in his head. He just began to paint, using the chance formations of the pigments as a substitute for forms in the external world and relying entirely on his intuitions. So the picture slowly arrived and the only problem was to decide when it was finished. The abstractionist art of Europe was different, for it had come out of Cubism and Mondrian and was based on the square and the circle, but the work of these American painters was open and fluid and usually demanded large canvases. It carried a strong emotional content, for it had its root in the loneliness of the New York artist camped down in a city of inhuman architecture in a country where there is no fellowship with or respect for physical objects, and so drew on a deep feeling of introversion that can almost be called religious.

Barnett Newman was in fact a Jewish mystic well versed in the Kabbala and his and Mark Rothko's enormous canvases, with all the pervading sensation they give of a dominant colour, produce on the viewer a powerful and almost hypnotic effect which one may well compare to a mystical experience, though Newman's word for it is 'the sublime'. Other painters, such as Jackson Pollock, attained rather different effects by pouring paint from a can and manipulating the forms it took, while Philip Guston, Robert Motherwell and Bradby Walker Tomlin used varying techniques. One might say that what this group has in common is the complete spontaneity of their painting and their almost metaphysical aim of reaching an absolute in which the viewer can lose himself. Thus he is not expected to look at the canvas as something that is outside himself, but to feel himself drawn into it and enveloped in it, as though he were in the interior of a great church or mosque. Hence most of their canvases are very large.

There is, I think, a grandeur about some of these paintings which puts them in a different category from the tighter and more limited works of the European abstractionists. They are very simple, they show nothing of what would normally be described as technical skill and nothing at all of the childish-seeming, pseudo-Freudian antics of the Surrealists. Instead they surge up from some deep layer on the borders of the unconscious and make a strong emotional impression, opening up in this way a new and entirely modern avenue for art. But an art which seems bound up with New York as the focussing point of that vast, formless, unreal country known as the United States.

‡ All art comes out of a technique for tapping the wells of the unconscious and subconscious. These wells are rich in feeling because they have not been deadened by the demands of daily life that visual experience should be reduced to the purely perfunctory. Without a limitation or blocking off of our sensory feelings we should not be able to conduct our lives, yet like seals that live under the Arctic ice we need some breathing holes where we can come up for air, and it is art more than anything else that provides these. Figurative art contains a frame of reference to the objects and experience of daily life, but it will not be a genuine art unless it draws its propelling and organizing impulse from some deeper level. It is from this impulse and not from its technical or repre-

sentational skill that it derives its power to lift us up and enhance our feeling for life. This may be the reason why the artist's personality is of less consequence to his work than in the case of the prose-writer or novelist, for, though conscious and deliberate in one part of his mind, he is likely to feel that he is principally a medium through which some deeper and less individualized current of feeling pours itself. The reasoning mind, if wrongly used, may thus become an obstruction, and one of the merits of abstract painting is that it can bypass it completely and seek like music to go to the centre of our being without, as Stravinsky said, having to make the detour of the brain. Most great art is, consciously or unconsciously, religious, because it reaches out towards ultimate things, and abstract art is often pre-eminently so because it has not been sifted through the welter of recognizable material objects, but aims at leading us directly, as the mystics do, to a state of imageless contemplation. Yet it does not follow from this that it is capable of producing the greatest masterpieces, since the path it takes is narrow and excludes any appeal to life-experience.

‡ We get the art we deserve. In the small communities of past ages life was full and animated and rich in human contacts. It took place in surroundings either of natural beauty or of splendid architecture. In the modern world of huge, sprawling conurbations with their faceless blocks of flats and their hurrying ant-like crowds and beetle traffic we lead diminished and impoverished lives. The larger the community, the more we sink back into our small individualities and lose our proper sense of belonging to a living social organism. It is true that our standard of education has risen greatly and that there are more people to be met with who have well-furnished and curious minds, but in spite of this our arts are dying because the world we live in is purposeless and emotionally dead. All one can say is that, such as they are, they help to redeem our circumstances – either by teaching us how to escape from them or by parodying them. Is there hope for the future? We may dream of better days to come, but no social or political system that we can think of will cure our state, because it is inherent in the conditions of an over-complex industrial and economic world with its swollen population that demands a high standard of material comfort to compensate for the increasing strain of life.

‡ The bad paintings of the past were pastiches of the academic art of the time, but today there is no academic art to copy, so that painters who lack creative talent try to make an impression by their originality or at least think that they must start off from some entirely new and capriciously chosen point. The consequence of this is that there has never been a period when more pretentious or extravagant paintings and sculptures have been produced and exhibited in galleries. Art styles have come to change as rapidly as styles in women's clothes so that a new look every year has become essential if a painter is to impress the gallery owners. The public becomes so dazed by these continually changing displays of artistic caprice that it ceases to trust to its own intuitions or to ask 'What does this picture do to me?'

‡ Music, as is often said, is the purest of the arts because it is only concerned with form. In all the other arts form is employed to organize visual or verbal material. That is to say, paintings and poems have a content, whereas music has none. Yet for many thousands of years music was used only to accompany dancing and singing: they gave it, one might say, its content till, with the invention of harmony and of an adequate system of notation, it burst out in the late Renaissance into a mature and self-sufficient art.

‡ Sound has a power of arousing emotion such as nothing else possesses. Its rhythms seem to act directly on the nervous system. It is for this reason no doubt that music is able to operate on some central point in our organism where all our feelings have their source, in a way which none of the other arts can do. Thus in listening to a sonata we are carried through a succession of complex emotions, enough to fill years of a life, in the space of half an hour. The range, the precision and the delicacy of our responses surprise us, for we did not know before that we had such a rich capacity for feeling or such nimbleness in moving from one mood to another under the mastery of that magical spell. Yet so poor is our language to express states of mind that we can only use such vague terms as gaiety, melancholy, humour or pathos to describe what we have felt. One would be inclined to say at once that music was the master art if one did not remember that it lacks one

immense thing that the other arts provide, which is a detailed context in our life experience. For music gives a finer texture to our emotional responses than our lives can ever give us: it offers us, one could say, a foretaste of that celestial Utopia on which we would like to think that a perfected humanity could one day plant its flag – but we live in a real world where our feelings are weighed down and entangled with gross circumstance, and music does not provide us with the solid fare we also need.

ARCHITECTURE

‡ Greek temple building was derived from Egypt with its column-like palm trees and its tradition of stone quarrying, but since the rise of Christianity there have been only two kinds of architecture in Western Europe – the Northern or Gothic and the Mediterranean. The first is an architecture founded on growth and living organisms and the second on geometry. Today the Mediterranean style has won everywhere because it is the most suitable for streets and houses. The last example of the Gothic style (apart from a few ultramodernistic French churches) is Gaudi's Sagrada Familia in Barcelona, which clearly reveals by its uncouthness and vulgarity how out of joint it was with its time.

‡ Great architecture is found only in those ages which had a strong religious or civic sense. It is naturally ostentatious and arrogant, for its purpose was to celebrate either the greatness of God or that of the community, or most often both together. But in the far more wealthy communities of today it has become strictly utilitarian and exists merely to serve some practical end. Modern states are the natural enemies of good architecture because, living only for material convenience and comfort and lacking in civic pride, they are not prepared to spend money on display. Perhaps, seeing the state to which architecture has been reduced, that is just as well.

‡ Some styles of architecture play on the force of gravity. Thus the Norman, which is a clumsy form of Romanesque, exemplifies

the pressure of heavy masses of stone weighing down on the earth, while the Gothic, which followed it, reacts against this impression and finally triumphs over it. For Gothic, which is Germanic in spirit though modified by French order and clarity, is all revolt and aspiration. With its pointed arches and clustered columns and fan vaulting it evokes the springing forces of vegetation, the rise of forest trees into the air, the spectacular liberation of earth-bound matter in a skyward ascent. In both cases there is an emphasis on the tremendousness of the force of gravity, either in the form of great masses of stone pressing downwards or of soaring columns, often topped by lace-work spires, that defy it. If this gravity can be said to stand for the load of misery and unredeemable sin that in the Dark Ages oppressed North-western Europe, then Gothic expresses the renaissance of the twelfth century with its resurgence of life and hope.

‡ One can say that Gothic architecture was developed from certain structural notions, such as the desirability of roofing churches by means of stone vaulting rather than with wooden beams which were apt to catch fire and burn. It went with a revolution in engineering and a better understanding of the laws of stress, which allowed the walls to be thinner and more space provided for windows which the new art of stained glass – the Western equivalent of mosaics – could fill. But one can also say that it soon came to exemplify a religious idea – the aspiration of men towards God and the ascent of their prayers to heaven. This idea made it seem more desirable to stress height than volume or space, with the result that to the classical Mediterranean mind the nave of Chartres Cathedral seems narrow and cramping, while the flying buttresses that counteract the outward thrust of the walls give the impression of scaffolding on an unfinished building. It was therefor not surprising that the Italians failed to seize the soaring spirit of Gothic and borrowed only its decorative elements, while the Catalan architects corrected it by broadening the arches of their naves so as to give a greater interior space as in Romanesque churches.

‡ Soon after Edward III came to the throne the bishop of Salisbury died and it became necessary to appoint a successor. Queen Philippa

wished her chaplain, Richard de Wyvile, to have the incumbency, but her husband objected on the ground that he was not only a dwarf but notoriously impotent, and on that account ought never to have been ordained. For according to canon law no one could be made a priest who was not physically whole and perfect. However the Queen persisted and got her way and the new bishop went down in 1329 to see his cathedral, which had been finished only some sixty years before. 'A magnificent building,' he exclaimed, 'but it lacks one thing. It has no spire. I will set to at once and build it the finest in England.'

‡ The Perpendicular is the only English Gothic style that is completely satisfying. It is as English as Chaucer or the Anglican Church, providing light and space rather than gloom and soaring height. But its name is a misnomer.

‡ The arch and the brick barrel vault were brought to Rome from the East some time in the first century and used in municipal buildings. Since pagan temples had not been intended to hold many people, the earliest Christian churches were built on the model of the basilica or court-room. The foundation of Constantinople in A.D. 330 marks the beginning of the orientalizing of the arts of the West, and the architectural consequence of this was the Byzantine style, which was the richest and most sophisticated that had yet been seen anywhere. As it spread westwards through Italy into France it lost much of its richness and sophistication, but developed its sense for space and volume, shown in its broad naves and central domes and cupolas. This was the style we vaguely call Romanesque and in its basic features of balance and good proportion it exemplifies the architecture of the Mediterranean.

The classic revival in Italy begins with Brunelleschi's vast dome in Florence with its billowing, bubble-like form that rises so amazingly in the centre of the city. This style, based on a study of Roman temples and on much mathematics, culminates in the work of Bramante and Raphael. Its aim was the attainment of perfect balance, harmony and elegance in all its parts. However it was not in the nature of such a delicate architecture to last in the conditions then prevailing in central Italy and it soon overbalanced into the massive, grandiose, rhetorical style of the Baroque which

with the fluidity and chiaroscuro of its façades fills Rome and
Umbria with its magnificence. St Peter's, which most people would
regard as the crowning monument of European architecture, comes
at the junction point between the two styles. But in the north of
Italy, where the Baroque hardly penetrated, the classic style continued to be used and reached its highest point of development in
the country houses and Venetian church façades of Palladio. Such
an explosion of great architecture, both religious and secular, has
never been seen in the world before and will most probably never
be seen again.

‡ 'Architecture has its political uses. Public buildings being the
ornament of a country, it establishes a nation, draws people and
commerce, makes the people love their country' (Sir Christopher
Wren, *Parentalia*). How many good buildings have been put up
since 1840 and how many pulled down?

‡ Sir Christopher Wren is no doubt the greatest of our architects.
What would London be without his churches? One can say that
many of our great country houses of this period are fine buildings,
but what seems to me to have been of more utility to the nation
is the simple but well-proportioned style in red brick that developed
in the reign of Queen Anne and was employed both for cottages
and farm houses and particularly for streets. Bedford Row in
London and many streets and squares in Dublin are some of the
few remaining examples of this. Nash and other architects continued
in a different but still excellent idiom to build city streets until the
Regency. It is difficult to remember today that in 1840 London
was the most beautiful and well-ordered city in Europe, if one
excepts its terrible slum areas, while now it is the ugliest. Wren
was right. Much of the philistinism of the Victorians must have
been due to the squalor of the buildings they daily looked at.

‡ Moslem architecture derives from the Byzantine. It relies for
its effects upon the simplicity and purity of its style and the
perfection of its proportions. On entering a mosque one gets a
feeling of air and space with the carpeted floor spreading round
one like a lawn and nothing to break the bareness of the white

walls but a single band of arabesque pattern in blue painted stucco which, when one looks at it fixedly, fascinates the eye by its complexity. The Arabs made of pattern and decoration something that by its regular recurrences affects the sense of sight as rhyme affects the ear in poetry. Their abnormal sensitivity to small variations of light, colour and spacing, and the dramatic quality of the Arabic script, enabled them to create patterns that in their endless, intricate returns of motif have an almost hypnotic effect. As in Arabic music, small variations on an ever-repeated theme lull the senses. But it is in the beauty and simplicity of its general proportions and in a certain sense it gives of emptiness and stillness that this architecture stands out.

Take for example the synagogue of the Tránsito in Toledo. This building is nothing more than an oblong box, seventy-five feet by thirty-one, with an arabesque frieze running round the upper walls and above it an arcade pierced with small windows. The roof is of coffered cedar, inlaid with ivory and mother-of-pearl plaques, and the sensation of cool delight and repose one gets on entering it is a proof of what can be done even in a small building by perfect proportions and lighting.

The architecture of the Ottoman Turks is of a very different kind, for it grew up in Istanbul under the shadow and influence of Justinian's great failure, Santa Sophia. In general it is heavy and insensitive, but it produced in Sinan, a Greek taken in childhood and brought up to be a Moslem janissary, one of the greatest architects of all time. His masterpiece is the enormous mosque at Edirne or Adrianople. In the power he there shows to create a vast domed space filled with light, as well in the classic delicacy and harmony of the details, he ranks with any architect in the world. What is astonishing is that he was brought up to be a military architect and bridge-builder and was past fifty when he built his first mosque.

Literature

‡ There is a simple rule for distinguishing between what is great poetry and what is not great poetry. Does one read it again and again? Does it affect us more the better we know it? Judged by this test, great poetry is something that occurs from time to time when good poets write verse. That is to say, it is hardly ever found continuously in long passages, and if it were it would stun and exhaust the reader.

‡ Poetry cannot be explained. It is just there. Critics, if they do not try too hard, can sometimes throw a little light on it, but they cannot tell us how or why it is good. For everything they write about a good poet would make equal sense if written about a mediocre one. They can treat Cowley as if he were Donne.

‡ A great deal of difficult or obscure poetry is published today because poets have come to feel that they can do more by suggestion than by direct statement. Yet unless a poem shows obvious signs of being well written, its obscurity will discourage many readers from attempting it. Some people may enjoy solving puzzles, but most read poetry to get immediate pleasure from it. Thus one may read every line that Hardy wrote (and most of his verse is weak) because its tone is sincere and its meaning transparent, whereas there are tracts of Donne's verse as well as passages in Shakespeare that fatigue one to no purpose. In private poets such as Sylvia Plath one is helped by the biographical notes, though the force and pungency of her verse comes through without them.

‡ People who inveigh against rhetoric in poetry are like those who tell conjurers that they ought not to make deceiving gestures. For while the tom-toms beat and the medicine man explains what he is going to do, the miracle happens.

‡ Rhetoric is to poetry what yeast is to bread: it makes it rise. The great age of rhetoric in England was the Elizabethan age and the splendour and bombast of its dramatic verse is comparable to the contemporary architectural style of the Roman Baroque, with its strong emphases, its fluidity and colour and its love of imposing façades. But in lyric poetry rhetoric is out of place because it is not the function of the lyric either to impress or to persuade. It still carries the marks of its origin as verse that was set to music.

‡ The style of conceits is the last great style in poetry to have swept through the whole of Europe. It began suddenly and almost simultaneously in Spain, England, Italy and France and then petered out slowly through the seventeenth century. The appearance of a similar style in Arabic poetry in the tenth and eleventh centuries shows that it is a natural phenomenon which occurs whenever poets, endowed with wit and a sharp eye, become bored with an idealizing or pastoral type of verse. Eliot, in his remarks on Donne and the 'objective correlative', missed the point through lack of a historical sense.

‡ The poet's or painter's business is to rescue things from the stream of becoming and fix them in the state of being. Thus if Heraclitus is the philosopher of living things, Parmenides can be called that of writers and artists. The poet or novelist must effect a transformation from the world of the one to that of the other. Or one can draw an analogy from Plato's forms or ideas. The form or universal governs a whole magnitude of things just as a good passage in a poem governs and so evokes a whole range of interlocked feelings and experiences.

‡ 'Eternity is in love with the productions of Time' (Blake).

‡ We are all of us lame or paralytic. The poet is the ballet-dancer who can move his limbs freely to the music, and when he does this something moves in us too.

‡ Imagination means letting the birds in one's head out of their cages and watching them fly up into the air.

‡ *Talent.* In the old Provençal or Limousin language talent (*talens, talans, talanz*) meant desire, longing, inclination. In Dante *talento* means lust. The change in the meaning of the word suggests that it is the strong desire to write or paint that creates the ability to do so.

‡ The bee, when it makes honey, believes that it is perpetuating the memory of the flowers that it has visited and which it is in love with. 'Hélène, quand vous serez bien vieille, le soir, à la chandelle,' it murmurs as it approaches them. But the larvae only notice that they are eating honey.

‡ Just as the dream elaboration is, according to Freud, an impromptu story thrown up to disguise something that cannot be avowed, so at the heart of many true works of the imagination there lies something dangerous and inadmissible. Compare the pearl that forms around a piece of grit that is irritating the oyster.

‡ On the flexibility of words. They bend and twist like branches in a wind in obedience to the rhythm and content. In poetry every word in a line modifies every other word and some of these words are capable of strange combinations.

‡ One of the marks of a great poet is that he creates his own family of words and teaches them to live together in harmony and to help one another. In this way each individual word gains a depth and richness of meaning it would not otherwise possess.

‡ Spenser is an example of a poet who only uses words that are on good terms with one another, just as Piero della Francesca only uses colours that accord among themselves. The language of his poetry has the purity and freshness of something that has just been born; it has the dew of early morning on it or, to change the metaphor, the look of having only yesterday risen out of a sea where it has been bathing in the original Platonic essences. It is for this reason that it lacks the dissonances and complexities of actual life. One consequence of this is that his principal poem, *The Faerie Queene*, in spite of its versification being always crystal clear and melodious and on the same level of excellence through-out, soon becomes monotonous. The story or allegory is, for us at least, merely something to hang the poetry on, for Spenser's ideas are not interesting.

‡ 'Words are the burden of poems, poems are made of words' (William Carlos Williams, *Peterson*, book 6). But the unit in poetry is not the word, but the sequence of words organized by the rhythm, which decides on their length, quantity and weight. Until the appearance of free verse with Whitman and Rimbaud this rhythm always fell into a particular pattern known as metre, but even in free verse the rhythm is supreme. Had Williams understood this he might have written better poetry.

‡ Is the image or the rhythm the basic thing in poetry? Take a good and striking image in a poem and rearrange its words in even the most trifling way and it will lose all its effect upon us. The two have been fused together to form a single indissoluble whole. If critics talk of poetry in terms of metaphors and images that is because there is no language in which poetic rhythm can be discussed. In music (when it is classical and not oriental) the rhythms can be analysed and noted down because they are relatively simple, but verse or speech rhythm is very complex. Its existence is usually therefore taken for granted by the critic or only referred to vaguely.

‡ There are some poets whose sense for rhythm is so strong that it carries everything before it. The most outstanding of these is

Swinburne. One of the features of his rapid, fluent rhythms is that they must often use words as counters to maintain their flow rather than as signs to convey meaning. Another is that their language tends to become charged with adjectives and double adjectives which help to fill out the line and which all point in the same direction. No pause for a qualification of the meaning is possible. Such insidiously flowing poems lend themselves to the diffusion of vague and dreamy moods rather than to the expression of feelings that are rooted in experience. Rhythms of this kind are very infectious and the masturbatory moods they inculcate tend to imprison poetry in a world of its own. In every branch of literature language must marry experience if it is to have any integrity.

One of the reasons for the long vogue of this kind of poetry in England is that till some time in the twenties it was chanted rather than recited, and this set up a sort of reverberation in the mind which made it impossible for the listener to distinguish good poetry from bad. Thus the diction became gradually more and more blurred by poetic overtones and adulterated by 'poetic' words so that down to the first decade of this century no poet could find a clean language to compose his verse in. The cure for this state of affairs required the appearance of a poet with intelligence and energy who had something of his own to say, for this would compel him to resist his rhythmical facility and hammer out a new and more direct idiom which would convey his true thoughts and feelings. (For in poets false language corrupts feeling just as false feeling corrupts language.) This is what Yeats did, just at a time when help was arriving from America. Eliot and Pound were the advance guard of General Pershing's divisions.

‡ Poetry is the result of a struggle in the poet's mind between something he wants to say and the medium in which he is trying to say it. The more resistant the medium, the more the poet's power and resilience will be called for, though if the form is too tight and restrictive, as it is in Provençal verse, most of what he wanted to say will have to be jettisoned. It is the failure to understand that poetry comes out of a struggle and requires power and energy to conduct that struggle, that makes so much contemporary verse flat and formless.

‡ *Contemporary poetry.* Sometimes I feel that there is a far-away country where much of the English poetry that is printed today was originally written. Our poets, without knowing the language well, translate it into that universal idiom known as translatese. Hence its lack of poetic rhythm, its inability to leave the ground. And when our poets do know how to write verse, they often pitch their tone very low as if to assure us that their lines will require no emotional response. It was Auden who, when his springs dried up, first let the Muse down by substituting technique for feeling.

‡ Poets are like dolls which need squeezing to get a good squeak out of them. A love-affair that turns bad, a dose of syphilis or TB, the death of a loved one. Even sin, that old dynamo, has lost much of its power since we have ceased to believe in Hell. A government that cared for poetry would clap all its poets in gaol and keep them there till they had a good book of verse ready.

‡ By what is known as inspiration is meant a sudden, unexplained access of power which opens up all those chambers of the mind that are usually sealed. The association of ideas becomes wider and more rapid, though often too superficially or chaotically to be of value. This state has been responsible for much good poetry as well as, in untrained or unprepared minds, some very bad poetry. But there are other states in which poetry can be written without any sense of power or stress because the poet's good fairies have prepared the way for him.

‡ When the grasshopper gathers its strength to hop, it does not know where it will land. So it often is with poets.

‡ *Vers donnés.* These are like the bubbles of marsh gas that rise from time to time from the bottom of a muddy pond. They are pure intuitions and come from the underground factory where poetry is brewed.

‡ Young poets might be well advised to try writing so-called nonsense poems in which all the nouns, adjectives and verbs are

invented. They might even find that they were their best poems.
As an example I will quote the first stanza of A. J. K. Wilkins'
lyric, *Portrait of My Mistress*:

> Incrustables emponged her gware.
> Pinguanas caracoled her seck.
> From her aureoled revair
> Catastoomed her frushwork greck.
> All was fingle, all was fleck
> In that mar of sconce brabair.

As Dr F. M. Tutman has pointed out in *New Frontiers*, this is
pure poetry, freed from the contaminating influence of allusion
and meaning, and he cites the last two lines as among the most
aesthetically sophisticated in English poetry.

‡ Lytton Strachey once said to me that Horace could not be a
good poet because everything he wrote was a platitude. This is
the Romantic view of poetry, for in fact it requires a very great
poet to make platitudes come alive, since they are sentiments we
once felt but, through the dulling of our minds by habit, have
ceased any longer to feel. The poet, through the power and
authenticity of his language, which derives from the freshness of
his response, revives them and so restores to us a part of ourselves
that we had lost.

‡ 'The genius bears the full weight of what is common and exists
hundreds and thousands of times over' (John Berger on Titian, in
A Painter of our Times).

‡ If a poet really believes, as Valéry, Eliot and Auden said they
did, that poetry is a superior sort of game, one must not expect
the greatest kinds of poetry from him. Great poetry can only be
written with a total conviction of its importance, and Auden knew
this till his powers began to fail. Eliot was copying Valéry.

‡ 'As the voice, passing through a trumpet, comes out sharper
and stronger, so the sense, compressed by the form of the poem,

issues suddenly and strikes us in a more vivid way (d'une plus vive secousse)' (Montaigne, *Essays*).

‡ A realization of the identical in different phenomena and of the differences in similar phenomena is, according to Plato, an important element in all philosophy. But in poetry it is supreme. Nothing delights the mind more than a good simile or metaphor. Is this because we like to think of all Nature and all our experiences in life as being at bottom related? Or is it not because the language of the subconscious, where the springs of poetry lie, consists of visual images and analogies and not of abstract ideas?

‡ 'Symbols are not signs or allegories for something we know. They seek rather to express an unconscious content whose nature can only be guessed at because it is still unknown' (Lars Pranger). Their importance would seem to lie in the fact that they draw energy out of the depths of the mind with which to organize and fuse together the elements they find in it. The process, as the reader knows, also works in reverse.

‡ Some of the minor literature of this century is that of 'gli accidiosi, spregando Natura e sua bontade'. Dante was right. Those who despise 'l'aer dolce che del sol s'allegra' are damned. When they write books they are the poisoners of the wells.

‡ Heraclitus said that one cannot step twice into the same river. Nor can one twice read the same book. Nor can other people read the same book that you have read. The good critic is the person who appears to have read the same book that you have, but who has plunged deeper into it.

‡ We are told that there should be more communication between the arts and the sciences. Certainly it is important for the writer to acquire some rough idea of what science has achieved and is achieving, because otherwise he will not belong to the modern world, while it is desirable that the scientist should have a feeling

for one or more of the arts or he will be in danger of having a two-dimensional mind. Everyone should aspire to being as human as possible and the pure rationalist can never be quite human because, as Wallace Stevens says, he has no shadow. But there is a limit to the time and energy that a person can give to matters that are outside his special sphere. Besides, no real understanding of the pure sciences is possible without some grasp of mathematics, and its atmosphere is so rarefied that few writers can breathe it.

‡ We seem to be coming to the end of a period of great literary criticism. Eliot started it off and, though his essays are sometimes marred by prejudice and blind spots, most of which he corrected later, he found more penetrating things to say about poetry than any English critic has done since Coleridge. Others have followed him along similar lines and if the end now seems near it is because the vein has been worked out. This flood of critical writing has done little to raise the level of our poetry or novels, but it has had an immense effect in sharpening the reader's response to literature. Indeed without the help of the critics much modern poetry would fail to produce its full effect upon us. We might get some enjoyment from it, but owing to the natural laziness of our minds, we would be doing so in the dark. Yet some of the most tedious and superfluous books ever written have come from the critics, owing to the fact that literature is now taught 'as a discipline' at universities and that anyone who wishes to get his Ph.D. can do so by writing upon it. Soon we shall be told that literary criticism is a science.

‡ To some contemporary critics a good poem is one that they can dissect and 'explicate'. What other reason, they seem to say, can there be for reading it?

‡ 'There is more effort required in interpreting interpretations than in interpreting poems, and more books come out upon books than on any other subject' (Montaigne, *Essays*).

‡ 'Great writers are significant in terms of the human awareness they promote' (F. R. Leavis, *The Great Tradition*). This is well said, but where poetry is concerned the most important thing is delight. Some great poets do no more to promote human awareness than do musicians. For instance, Spenser, Marlowe in his *Hero and Leander*, and Wallace Stevens.

‡ 'On a certain low level we judge by precepts and by art. But the great, the excessive, the divine are above the rules of reason' (Montaigne, *Essays*).

‡ What is detestable in some critics of poetry is their way of laying down the law and telling us which poets we may read and which we may not. Our choice of reading is our own affair and if we have a genuine feeling for poetry we are just as likely as they are to make a good one. We read the critics because they have given more time and thought than we have to the poets they are discussing and so can be helpful, but in the end our own judgement is the only one that should count for us. Poetry exists to be enjoyed and not minutely dissected and if we know too much about a poem we are likely to enjoy it less. The best critics illustrate their points with ample quotations so that we may judge for ourselves. But how many good critics of poetry have there been in the past fifty years? At the most a dozen.

‡ The mood in which we read poetry should be a passive and receptive one in which our critical and intellectual faculties are subordinated to our immediate feeling. Therefore no 'close reading'. Good poetry must get into our bloodstream before we stop to examine it. Then, when we later meditate on a passage we have liked, a fuller understanding of its meaning and relevance to us will come out. This is sound Taoist doctrine, as several anecdotes by Chuang Tzu show, and Eliot approved of it.

‡ Critics should write for lovers of poetry rather than for practising poets. Hence Dr Leavis' howler over Milton. It is absurd to say that Milton is not a very great poet, but it is not absurd to say

that in a certain period he might be a bad one for young poets to read. Thus Blake and Wordsworth had to demolish Pope and his stopped couplets before they could begin to write their own poetry. Yet, when a poet has once established his style, Milton should be a great educator for the ear, even though like Pope he wrote in a manner that is remote from ours. Brancusi much admired Michelangelo and declared that he had learned everything from him.

‡ One should never embark on a poem with a previous idea of what it ought to be. This is the mistake that Johnson made when he condemned *Lycidas*, which most people would consider to be one of the two or three most beautiful poems in English. Apart from the fact that he had little ear for poetry and approached it chiefly from the side of morality and common sense, he did not understand the convention of the pastoral. This is a kind of poetry that refuses to take its supposed subject too seriously, but which under the mask of describing the fictional life of shepherds, for which it had a precedent in Greek and Latin, gets nearer to the 'pure poetry' of our time than anything else its age could manage. Some of the greatest Spanish and Italian poets of the Renaissance followed this convention, as does of course much of the painting, and perhaps one could say that Wallace Stevens' poetry has affinities with it. The taste for classical and Biblical allusions that Milton exemplified in his similes, and which served the purpose of drawing on the poetic reservoirs of the past and so deepening and extending the significance of what was being said, has been revived in our time in a more devious way by Pound and Eliot. Such allusions to past poetry were of course a very important element in classical poetry as well as in that of the Arabs and Chinese. Our present taste for a poetry that comes stark and direct from life may be more appropriate to an age that lives with its nose in the drains and that lacks both leisure and learning. But Eliot gave us both and Pound in his *Cantos* tried to.

‡ By a good prose style is meant a clean and clear flow of language, not overloaded with qualifying words or clauses and moving with a certain current. It should have some personal flavour and yet conform to ordinary usage. It is his failure to do this last that

makes Carlyle so irritating to read in spite of his imaginative gifts and his occasional ability to throw out a striking phrase. A nice judgement of the values of adjectives and adverbs is also expected of a good writer and one of the marks of the best lies in his choice of epithets. Eccentric or poetical styles such as those of Sir Thomas Browne, de Quincey or Doughty belong to a different category, while Donne is an orator rather than a prose writer.

‡ 'Le style est à lui seul une manière absolue de voir.' 'Style is in itself an absolute way of seeing' (Flaubert, *Lettres à Louise Colet*, January 1852). This equates prose style with poetry as a medium for giving a total impression, but there are less ambitious styles that aim only at clarity and transparency. Thus George Orwell says that a good prose style is like a window-pane, and Jules Renard that clarity is the politeness of the man of letters. André Gide's *Journal* is a fine example of writing of this sort, which reaches perfection and more than perfection in French literature of the age of Louis XIV.

‡ A really good prose style is like a good wine: it gives a special pleasure to the cultivated palate. Yet one can get drunk on bad wines and many admirable novels lack distinction of language.

‡ The best styles in either prose or verse are those in which words have retained some of their subconscious associations: that is to say, they constitute a real and complete language and not the castrated one in which we most of us most of the time communicate with one another.

‡ When a novelist makes his characters talk he should remember that people convey what they mean as much by their changes of tone and facial expressions as by the words they use. He must therefore find in the style of speech he gives them an equivalent for this without having always to describe it. In this difficult art Kingsley Amis is a master.

‡ Many so called primitive languages have refinements that European languages lack. Thus some American Indians divide the past tense into a recent past, a remote past and a mythological past. Without venturing too far into the dark forest of linguistics, we may come across many grammatical forms that we should be glad to possess. English, for example, lacks a pronoun such as the French *soi* or *son* to stand for *him-or-her*, although such a word cries out to be born. When our modesty impels us to use the impersonal pronoun *one*, we have to follow it up with a string of cacophonous *one*s. But English is the language of an increasingly inarticulate people who are incessantly eroding and blurring the finer distinctions in the idiom they have inherited. Thus the subjunctive mood has almost ceased to exist while such words as *yonder*, so characteristic of a country-dwelling people, have been dropped. With it has gone the dialect word *yonderly*, which is much more expressive than *absent-minded*. Dozens of other cases of such throwings overboard of expressive words could be given, and writers have been hard put to it to keep the language properly stocked. The great falling-off began in Victorian times, because industrialism destroys the culture of the masses while the press emasculates that of the middle class.

‡ Wordsworth claimed to base his poetry on the language of ordinary men. But this language has been in a state of rapid decay since people began to read the daily newspapers and the cheap novels and magazines that sprang up with them. A language is usually spoken best by men and women who have not acquired the habit of reading and who confine their conversation to matters that they thoroughly feel and understand. But today everyone reads and so is exposed to those examples of slovenly writing that circulate everywhere as well as to ideas and concepts that they only half grasp. Good talkers have therefore become rare, even in pubs. For this reason a special responsibility is thrown on writers to preserve the purity and vitality of the language and keep at arm's length the pseudo-scientific jargons that are rapidly infiltrating it.

‡ Some of the best prose writers of this century have been the philosophers – Collingwood, James, Russell, Santayana, Wisdom,

Ayer and Ryle. But the extreme clarity and precision of the styles of these last three are not appropriate to literary usage, which requires that the meanings of words should not be clipped but allowed to keep their rough edge of associations.

‡ A certain crispness in a style is a valuable quality. Voltaire had it to a supreme degree and so sometimes had Bertrand Russell. It is a mark of precision and hardness of mind. Words are used to cut. Then there are the writers who write well because they are complete masters of the material in their heads, however limited this may be. Bernard Shaw is one of these, and his *Intelligent Woman's Guide to Socialism and Capitalism* is a very well-written book although the subject is as boring as are his plays. But for sheer beauty of style no English book comes up to Newman's *Apologia*.

‡ The style of Montaigne reflects more closely than any other the mind of a man feeling his way in words and ideas. It is an open style, twisting and winding as his thought grows and develops, both subtle and precise at the same time. Also it is the mode of expression of one of the most adventurous and enquiring minds that any writer has ever possessed. Montaigne speaks to every age provided one reads him in his own language and not in Florio's translation, which gives an impression of quaintness that French prose, which unlike the English of that time was a mature idiom, had left behind.

‡ The eighteenth century was the great age for English prose styles as the seventeenth had been for the French: writers then stand out from one another as much by their manner of writing as by their subject matter. Thus one gets (a little earlier) the easy, armchair style of Dryden, the hard metallic one of Swift with his patter of monosyllables, the artificial style of long periods employed by Gibbon, the mincing one of Addison, the vigorous, majestic yet rough one of Dr Johnson. This is the age of 'le style c'est l'homme'. One of the most original is that of Sterne's *Sentimental Journey*. This book is all style – a flow of language that follows the writer's constantly changing mood and fits it like a glove. It has a freedom of movement that suggests a dance, but

a very extraordinary dance, all lightness of step and pirouettes and display like the courtship dances of certain sea-birds. One would call it an affected style if there was any substance behind it, but there is none. Unlike *Tristram Shandy* ,which has solid qualities, it is all thistledown and exists for the sake of the performance alone.

‡ The cliché is dead poetry. English, being the language of an imaginative race, abounds in clichés, so that English literature is always in danger of being poisoned by its own secretions. French, on the other hand, being a language more given to abstractions, contains fewer of these poisons, which makes it a better language for purposes of exposition. A great deal of the beauty of the French style lies in the precision of its syntax, which is today, in writers such as Sartre, being eroded. Yet it is a mistake to think that clichés should never be used by good writers. Since their meaning is so familiar they can, if well chosen, provide a rest for the mind and give a more leisurely movement to the sentence. Similarly it is not true that every word or expression needs to be clear and exact. A good deal can be done by words that are vague and plastic: consider the use that Vergil makes of the word *res*.

‡ It is much too simple to say, as Buffon did, that a writer's prose style is a reflection of his character. It is often much more closely related to the ease or otherwise with which he expresses himself. Some writers, such as Goldsmith, have a natural flow of language which conveys immediately what they wish to say, while others are not satisfied with such easy expression, supposing that they have it, but adopt a more artificial idiom which either condenses or emphasizes their intentions. As examples of this one may take Tacitus and Flaubert. The case of Henry James's last period is especially revealing. The circumlocutory, parenthetic, procrastinating style that he adopted after 1897 is the result of an impediment, such as a psychiatrist might be able to explain, which in conversation prevented him from saying the simplest thing briefly and directly. Such a style, taken as style, is obviously diseased, though some of his admirers claim that it suited the purpose of his later novels because in them he was concerned with adumbrating the finest shades of meaning which any brute statement of fact would have

shattered. His brother William, who was perhaps the best American prose writer since Jonathan Edwards, failed to see this and most readers will agree with him.

‡ 'The light of high narrowish French windows in an old room, the light somehow, as one feels, of 'style' itself' (quoted by Leon Edel from Henry James). This is exactly what I have often felt – the connection between the high windows of old French houses and good, clear, severely written French literature.

‡ The mistaken belief that prose styles are better in proportion as they employ fewer adjectives and adverbs is due to the fact that energetic styles discard as many supernumerary words as possible in order to move more rapidly. One of the chief uses of adjectives is to reduce the speed and allow the mind, by a more leisurely progress, to draw richer impressions. The most rapid of all narrative styles is that of Voltaire in his *Contes*, but he uses great selection and abstraction to achieve this. The most leisurely styles are those of de Quincey and Proust.

‡ 'Autobiography is a literary form like any other – something between biography and novelizing. The one because controlled by actuality, the other because it can be seen from within, through memory' (Eckermann, *Conversations with Goethe*). Since memory was for Goethe a creative rather than a recording faculty, his autobiography departs widely from the facts.

‡ The most tedious of museums or book collections would be one dedicated to the avant-garde literature of every age. It would contain very few great names, whereas if paintings were included it would contain a great many.

‡ Pope made poetry out of society as Chaucer had done in a broader way: Wordsworth, inspired by Rousseau and the Cambridge Platonists, took his inner experience and made a philosophy out of it. The one delights us by his sharp observations of men and

by his exquisite feeling for language, the other exhilarates and lifts up the mind in spite of his often flat-footed diction. But language is what lasts longest in poetry: when it is as precise and as perfectly phrased and as kind to the ear as is Pope's it never stales, so that one is apt to turn to him rather than to Wordsworth after the force of the latter's message has exhausted itself.

‡ It is not altogether just to say that Wordsworth grew reactionary as he grew older. Since (like Robespierre) he took his main ideas from Rousseau, he believed that men grew to a greater moral stature in the country than in the city. His political idealism therefore took the form of wishing to see a rural society of prosperous smallholders and farmers. When after a time he realized, what Shelley and most of the Romantics were blind to, the misery brought on by the Industrial Revolution, he turned to the party of the large landowners who at least clung to the duties on corn upon which the prosperity of agriculture depended. Had he been a less inwardly directed man he might have visited Manchester and found a new theme there for his poetry.

‡ On listening to Eliot's *Cocktail Party* on the radio. I don't like to see great poets writing down to their audience. Even when they do it as well as they can, they still do not do it well enough.

‡ We are sometimes told that Milton wrote his poems in a Latinized idiom that is contrary to the spirit of the English language. But in what sort of an idiom did Vergil and Horace write? Surely in one that was very remote from common speech and with a highly artificial word order. It seems more likely that Milton developed his style because it accorded not only with his personal character and mode of feeling but with the sublimity of his subject matter. Latinized or not, the style of *Paradise Lost* and *Samson Agonistes* *is* Milton.

‡ Poets usually dry up as they grow old, though some of the greatest have been exceptions. Thus Stesichorus, Anacreon, Simonides, Pindar and Sophocles were all going strong in their eighties,

and the last composed his *Philoctetes* at the age of eighty-seven. We later races have not done so well because we lead less healthy lives under less stimulating conditions, but Milton was writing great poetry in his sixties, and Yeats in his seventies. Then there are the poets whose Muse deserts them early, but who at long intervals throw off a notable poem. Tennyson was one of these, for having ceased to write anything worthwhile by the time he was forty-six, he suddenly at the age of seventy-two wrote his poem *To Virgil* at the request of the Podestá of Mantua. It is not only one of his most beautiful poems, but one of his few intelligent ones, since it contains the finest criticism of Vergil ever written. He composed his lovely lines to Catullus at the same time. Wordsworth too, after twenty years of dull but copious verse, had a brief revival in his moving poem on the death of James Hogg.

‡ Until recently I took the greatest novels by British writers to be *Middlemarch* and *Wuthering Heights*, but then I re-read *Vanity Fair*. If the principal aim of the long novel is to display human character and relationships in all their various twists and turns as they operate in society, then I would say that no book in any language has accomplished this with greater fidelity to nature than Thackeray's masterpiece, though with an emphasis on the moral side that limits its scope. Yet for all the skill shown by the plot in sustaining suspense and the subtle and convincing way in which the characters are made to evolve and develop, the book lacks something because it does not, like *Anna Karenina*, create the full illusion of life. Thackeray sees everything from outside.

Then there is Dickens, who is surely in creative force our greatest novelist. His enormous faults and lapses prevent many people from re-reading him – we have all made his acquaintance in childhood – but, if we do, the sharpness of his eye and the vividness of his mythopoeic imagination carry everything before them. His limitations are that his mind is almost entirely extroverted and his views on life shallow and jejune, yet when he lets his imagination go he passes beyond these, for there is a poet inside him. He is a writer for the innocent eye since he provides no moral living space for his characters, who are all two-dimensional, but just with stupendous force and dramatic energy calls them up before us and makes them live.

‡ One does not, I think, connect the word greatness with Jane
Austen since her range of subject and experience is so limited.
She does not stretch our imaginative capacity as all the great
novelists and dramatists do, since nearly every scene in her books
is pleasing: it is chiefly the nicer shades of our moral sensibility
that she stimulates. Yet she is the most accomplished artist of the
novel that perhaps any literature has produced. Her plots and her
characterization and her style of writing are all perfect, and though
she only touches on the deeper feelings and passions, she is a
master of comedy. She has further such an absolute sureness of
judgement that a single chapter by her will tell us more of the
finer points of human character and conduct than many chapters
by other writers. For this reason there is no English novelist
whom one can re-read so often, for the perfection of her writing
gives her work some of the attributes of poetry. Her death at the
age of forty-two is one of the disasters of English literature, for
further experience of life would have widened her scope and
deepened her vision.

‡ And what of Henry James? By the time he was forty-five he had
produced more than half a dozen novels and stories that rank
with any written in English, of which *The Portrait of a Lady*,
The Bostonians, Daisy Miller and *The Aspern Papers* are the most
outstanding. For psychological subtlety, social sophistication and
skill in storytelling they surpass anything written in that century,
though they lack the solidity and feeling of being rooted in the
soil that are shown by the novels of many English writers. There
is something a little thin-spun and diaphanous about all of them.
Then in the novels of the next ten years James's increasing obsession
with technique and his gradual alienation from reality lead, in
spite of much display of brilliance, to an effect of virtuosity and
tour-de-force. That is to say, one admires, but is neither convinced
nor moved.

Finally, towards 1899, his lack of hold on reality and his tendency
to shy away from any direct statement of fact assume much larger
proportions and one becomes aware, both in the records of his
conversation and in his writing, of a loosening of grip. This is
the period of *The Ambassadors, The Wings of the Dove* and *The
Golden Bowl*, which some of his admirers regard as his finest
books. In them the characters are less clearly defined: it is their

relations that matter most and these are elaborated at great length in his slow, circumlocutory manner. They are permeated by a sense of the evil produced by money, which adds to their heavy, sinister quality. But I have to admit that I find these books very tedious to read, both on account of their long-winded style and of the suffocating, hothouse atmosphere that one enters if one persists in hacking one's way through their thicket of overloaded sentences.

‡ Opinions are divided about Virginia Woolf's novels. Personally I have never been able to get on with them. Her decision to experiment with a new kind of novel that by treating the characters mainly from the inside and eliminating plot and action would produce a closer picture of reality, leads inevitably to the loss of that expectation as to what is going to happen next that is the backbone of all fiction and gives it its tension. And it is this loss that I complain of in her novels. Scattered with beautiful images, touched with fantasy, sceptical and ironical, they express her personal vision, which is largely an aesthetic one, with something of the passage of time in it which gives them an undercurrent of sadness. It is the vision of a poet rather than of a novelist, a sort of dramatized meditation on life, and for that reason lacks what would seem to be a necessary constituent of all true novels – that is, the moral element, which can only be brought out by the interaction of one character on another. This I miss. My taste, rightly or wrongly, inclines me to stronger meat – for example to the novels of a far lesser writer, Ivy Compton Burnett, with their splendid sense for evil.

Yet I am a great admirer of Virginia Woolf's work in general. In nearly everything she wrote she showed that rare quality of the imagination we call genius. I recognize this best in her essays on literary subjects that are contained in *The Common Reader* and in subsequent volumes. One could call many of these essays a triumph of articulacy, for they flow with great ease in a clear, lively idiom that reads like very good conversation, and yet convey a fine perception of their subject and a wide range of taste. This makes them perfect appetizers to the books they treat of. Finally there is her *Journal*, which gives a moving account of the doubts and agonies of the creative writer, exacerbated in her case by shattering headaches and the threat of insanity.

‡ So far as form goes, P. G. Wodehouse can be called the Jane Austen of our age. Like her he showed in his better novels a perfect sense for plot, a perfect style and a perfect though limited sense for comic situation and character. Only he did not write about real life but about a world that, even when he was young and contributed funny sketches to boys' magazines, was entirely fanciful, so that, since truth to life is such an important element in the novel, he must be placed in a much lower category. Yet his Bertie Wooster, Jeeves and Aunt Agatha will live on over the years as symbols and caricatures of the English class system, much as Oblomov does of the Russian, while the equally symbolic and much more actual and relevant Tommy Handley and his wartime circus are already forgotten, even though as radio figures their performances can be repeated. Only the written word persists. All other media are as ephemeral as are Grimaldi, Dan Leno, Little Tich and even Charlie Chaplin, although they had a greater genius than Wodehouse and spoke to us more directly. Marshall McLuhan is wrong. Mild, slow-paced literature always wins in the end.

‡ Sometimes a writer of talent appears from nowhere, publishes a book or two and vanishes. Such was Dorothy Edwards, whose volume of short stories, *Rhapsody*, followed by a novel, came out in 1927. They are books that have a special flavour that is unlike anything else. To begin with they are all concerned with music and musicians and the narrator is in each case a man. Then they are written in a deliberately simple style with great narrative skill in a technique she had worked out for herself in reaction to what she regarded as the lack of subtlety of English story-writing. Although little happens in most of them they make a lasting impression because of their uncanny power of conveying atmosphere. Their theme could be described as loneliness, people drifting together and drifting apart and unable to make themselves known to one another. Music is the one consolation.

Dorothy Edwards was a Welsh schoolmistress who, though she had travelled and spoke several languages, showed no sign when one met her of her rare talent. Then in 1931 she killed herself. The only person to have written of her is David Garnett in the third volume of his autobiography, *The Familiar Faces*. Since she was an ardent Welsh Nationalist it would seem that some of her compatriots might consider republishing her two books, if possible with some account of her life and ideas on writing as recorded in her letters. Modern Welsh literature is not so rich in talent that it can afford to neglect such a fine artist.

‡ One of the most original and stimulating novels of this century is *The Confessions of Zeno* by Italo Svevo. This is the nom-de-plume of an Italian industrialist from Trieste and much of the novel's freshness and originality are due to its being outside any literary tradition. It is a book steeped in an irony of the Viennese kind, gay, though on speaking terms with sadness, and with a philosophy of life that contradicts the values of the solemn puritan North. Since it first appeared in English in 1930, I have made a practice of lending my copy to friends and giving them a black mark if they do not like it.

‡ On reading *Big Sur* by Henry Miller. No one who does not understand that by literature is meant bringing order where before there was vagueness and disorder can have much conception of what that word means. Miller is not really a writer but a non-stop talker to whom someone has given a typewriter. Yet, as a sign of the times, of what young Americans are doing and thinking today, his book has an interest. Perhaps too, in this rootless, floating world of hippies and pot smokers, it is, like Ginsberg's poetry, the first step towards the literature of the future, of the approach of the Dark Ages when the universities will have shrunk into themselves and the only real art will be popular art, as it was in the eighth century.

‡ *Nabokov.* The case of Nabokov reminds me of that of Apuleius. Both of them learned the language they were to write in from tutors and only acquired a competent knowledge of it in their twenties. Both of them showed an astonishing talent for manipulating it, which so went to their heads that they became more and more precious in their style and subject matter. Who, for example, among English writers of talent could have written a serious poem on dentifrice, as Apuleius did, except Nabokov? And in their use of erotic subjects for unerotic ends they are also similar. Unlike other Russian writers Nabokov lacks that moral passion which

would give him a sense of purpose and direction, but he could do a wonderful free translation of Gogol's *Dead Souls*.

‡ Balzac thought himself a realist who was mapping out the new class, the bourgeoisie, that had come to the front after the French Revolution, and most people, including Karl Marx, have agreed with him. But in fact there is a strong tinge of melodrama in his novels, some bad romantic writing and large tracts which fail to convince because he did not know the society he was describing sufficiently well. He spent too much time at his writing desk to have an experience of life commensurate with the range of his novels, and it was only the provincial life of the Loire valley that he was thoroughly familiar with. Then, though gifted with a prodigious industry and an obsessive imagination, he shows only a moderate psychological penetration into his characters and there is a certain coarseness in his perceptions which is reflected in his colourless style. Yet on account of the huge scope and novelty of his undertaking and the vigour of some of his books, he must be regarded as a great novelist in spite of the fact that, like Hugo, he had no point of view of his own.

‡ *Stendhal.* One may question whether Stendhal is to be called a great or even a very good novelist, though both *Le rouge et le noir* and *La Chartreuse de Parme* contain brilliant and highly original scenes as well as some absurd and unconvincing ones. His fascination lies in his own complex character and in his idiosyncratic attitude to life. A Romantic in his feelings and a Voltairean in his ideas, he spun out of himself a very personal philosophy which he called 'Beylisme'. It is this that makes everything he wrote – his novels, his journals and his letters – of interest to those who feel drawn to him. The autobiography of his early years, *La vie de Henri Brulard*, is a little masterpiece, yet if his other books had not been there to sustain it, it would be nothing, for it is a strictly private document written only to please himself. His programme of enlightened egotism, which he called 'la chasse au bonheur', marks a step forward in self-consciousness and is a refreshing contrast to the moral attitudes of most English writers. So is his worship of energy rather than of virtue, his admiration of passion, even when it leads to *crime passionnel* or brigandage, and his love

of self-analysis. Like his contemporary Benjamin Constant, who in a duller way resembles him, he prided himself on being above everything a psychologist. It was Italy that formed him, and made him, though a witty conversationalist, little appreciated in Paris. As a writer he was an amateur in a nation of professionals, a man with whom one must identify, down even to his vanity and his absurdities, if one is to like him, but whom one may then feel more strongly drawn to than to any other French prose writer of that century. For in spirit he belongs to ours.

‡ *Flaubert*. D. H. Lawrence said that Flaubert was a man who hated human beings. That is not true. What he hated was what he called the bourgeois, by which he meant the man of mediocre mind, shallow views and low instincts, whatever his social class might be. On this subject he was fanatical. Yet how tender and compassionate is his portrait of Charles Bovary, whom he made one of the dullest and most insignificant of men! Or that of Félicité in *Un coeur simple*!

Flaubert's disease, as one might call it, was to find the life of his time mean and unsatisfying because, like a Jansenist of the seventeenth century, he had a high conception of what life ought to be. This ideal, he thought, lay in the past before the steam-roller of order and progress had flattened peoples' minds into their present flimsy and two-dimensional shapes. Such a belief, living as he did in that age, made him a Romantic, so that when he decided to write about contemporary life he chose as his leading figure a woman who, though limited, shallow and egotistic, was a Romantic too and destroyed herself because she thought she had been born for something better than what fate had given her. It was no doubt an impoverishing and life-denying creed for a novelist to adopt but, like the hermits of past ages, Flaubert was an all-or-nothing man who felt that he had seen through the illusions of life and could only find salvation in art, of which he made a religion. So to that he devoted himself and to his crusade against the stupidity and pretentiousness of his age, every year with greater fanaticism.

‡ *Madame Bovary* is no doubt the greatest French novel. It is a book that leaves out nothing. We are shown the dull Norman

landscape in all its seasonal phases, we enter into the petty affairs of a small provincial town and we see whenever we need to see through Emma Bovary's eyes. Both her and her husband's biographies are traced in detail from the cradle to the grave. It is a dense, one could almost say a relentless book. Every space is filled in, every 'i' is dotted, nothing is left to our imagination. It has the solidity, the concreteness, the monumental quality of a great poem, all the more because there is so much weight and sonority in the writing, which has every good quality except spontaneity.

Yet as we read we are very aware of being only spectators. Something, perhaps the barrier of a too organized prose, comes between us and the actors. Still more, we realize that Flaubert has distanced them from us by showing us that they are members of a society that he despises. Thus, though in Emma Bovary he has created one of the most complete and sensitive portraits of a woman in the whole of literature, we cannot identify with her as we do with Anna Karenina because we find her attitude to life too superficial. The author's crushing sense of the futility of the contemporary scene eats into our valuation of the characters. This is the price that he has paid for his conscientious objectivity and his laboriously achieved style. We read this most artistically perfect of novels with admiration and even with delight, yet we are left with a cold, dead feeling at the end as though we had been looking at the world through the wrong end of a telescope.

Yet one can read *Madame Bovary* in another way, as an epic poem to dullness – not only the dullness of the life of the small towns but of the Norman countryside with its rolling slopes, its dusty roads, its coarse grass, its placid cows, where the seasons mutate according to a fixed pattern and acquire by their invariable routine a sort of Parmenidean beauty. It is the dullness too of the heavy Norman nature, so different to that of the Ile de France, and of that stolid, phlegmatic Corneille who is its most characteristic writer. But Flaubert was aware of and impatient with this dullness which extended for him through the whole of northern France, wherever the bourgeoisie led their shallow lives, and in *Bouvard et Pécuchet* his anger against it reaches such a point of obsession that he becomes himself one of their partners. It even spills over into *Salammbô*, where his heavy set-pieces create it, though in *Saint Julien l'Hospitalier* it is absent. Here his romantic feeling for the Dark Ages leads to a piece of poetical writing which far outclasses Chateaubriand's *Atala*, that preposterous book which had been with Montesquieu the chief influence in the formation of his style. On this style Proust contributed a very enlightening article to the *Nouvelle revue française*.

‡ Proust is the novelist and poet of the interior life. The rhythms of his prose reproduce the systole and diastole of the emotional stream – the movement towards the desired object or state and the withdrawal from it again in failure or disillusion. He creates few if any characters in the round. What for example do we know of Madame de Guermantes when she is not making rather poor *bons mots* in a salon? His personages are mostly two-dimensional figures, recognizable from the outside, but not intimately realized because his method of centring them on the narrator precludes this. As one volume succeeds another they grow and change and form surprising combinations, thus giving us a sense of the passage of time and of the mutability of things, which is after all the author's principal theme. For this book is not in the usual sense of the word a novel, but a spiritual autobiography, in which the narrator is more or less identical with the author, though the characters have been combined and changed from their real-life originals. To appreciate it one must therefore be able to identify completely with the narrator. This becomes more difficult in later life, so that, if one re-reads it then, one will be bored by many of the passages and even by whole volumes that once held one spellbound. This is especially the case with the Albertine episode, which is only acceptable to someone who is living through a similar situation and even then does not ring entirely true because the original of Albertine was a boy. Great therefore though this book is, both for the beauty and the humour of many of its passages and for the high level of intelligence it shows throughout, it is doubtful if it can be regarded as a classic – that is, as a book that will keep its value intact in every age – as for example *War and Peace* and *Anna Karenina* are certain to do. But what it has done is to extend the frontiers of the articulate as no literary work has done since Montaigne's *Essays*, or Murasaki's *Tale of Genji* for the Japanese, and so has enormously increased our sensitivity to our environment. We are never the same person again after reading it.

‡ *On re-reading Racine.* On reading through his plays one after the other I was struck once again by their narrowness, which is really the penetrating narrowness of the French seventeenth-century mind taken up with its two obsessive themes of love and *gloire*, or reputation, and restricted further by the severe rules of French prosody. But the perfection of their construction is without parallel and with this goes a fine psychological sense. Yet what I read him most for is the beauty of the diction. Racine's poetry differs from all other kinds of poetry in seeming to be, not an expansion or flowering of thought or feeling, but a distillation of the simplest and purest language. It is muted poetry and all the more memorable and haunting on that account. No other French poet except Villon or Baudelaire ploughs so deep a furrow. And no other poet except La Fontaine shows such an economy of language.

‡ There is always a mythological element in tragedies. As Racine said in his preface to *Bajazet*, 'One may say that the respect one has for the hero grows in proportion to his distance from us.'

‡ *Rimbaud.* I first read Rimbaud when I was nineteen and for some eight years he was, with Blake, my favourite poet. Much of his verse and prose are very obscure, but I took the passages that suited me and made what I could of them. Some of them acquired a deep personal meaning for me. Then twenty-five years later I read Enid Starkie's admirable book on him and other books by French writers. By this time his occult and alchemic symbolism had been fully worked out and nearly everything that had previously been obscure became clear. I found this interesting because it led me to a better understanding of his inner life, but it did not affect my appreciation of his poetry because the occult means nothing to me. I still continued to read it for what it had given me before. I put this down because it provides an illustration of the way in which obscure poetry works on the reader and of how little a full interpretation of it can give him. This is also true in the cases of Gérard de Nerval and Mallarmé.

Rimbaud seems to me essentially a poet for the young, who understand him intuitively in a way that older people cannot. His verse and prose are a record of his adolescent *rites de passage*, which ended with his acceptance of reality. After that he judged them with his reason and found them nonsense, as all poetry is when read in that way. What then is meant by obscurity in poetry? In most poems the rational element is merely the framework for something that cannot be analysed or grasped by the rational mind. That is to say, all poetry is obscure because the prose meaning does not convey the full meaning, which derives from the unconscious and is untranslatable into other words.

‡ English novels are tied up in their petty class values, French novels are influenced by literary theories – what a relief then to turn to the Russians, who seem to breathe a fresher and more natural air! Yet Tolstoy's two great novels are Western in spirit with little that is specifically Russian about them, while *War and Peace* is a historical novel which has been given a contemporary tone. Turgenev's *Sportsman's Sketches* reads like the experiences of an English snipe-shooter in the Irish bogs. To get the full Russian flavour one must read Gogol, Dostoyevsky, Leskov, Schedrin and Gorky. And then there is Chekhov. Both in his plays and in his later stories he displays an awareness of the inner life and of human relationships that makes everything that has been written in England since that time seem coarse and crude.

‡ *Tolstoy.* I first read Tolstoy's *Sebastopol* in the winter of 1915–16 when I was living in a French village not far behind the front line, and was amazed at the truth and vividness with which he conveyed the experience of modern war. Then I read *War and Peace.* The enormous scale of this book gave me a feeling about fate and history and the lives of nations and individuals which helped me to see in better perspective the war I was engaged in. It was not entirely vile. There was a grandeur as well as a horror about it, as there must be whenever Fate shows itself openly in a large way.

It was a Russian writer who put these consoling ideas in my head, and no one else could have done it because he gave me not a mere novel, much less an argument, but a panoramic view that in its truth to life was utterly convincing. It was more real, more true in its account of what things are like than any other book I had read. And that is what I still feel today. By his amazing power of putting himself inside other people and so reading their thoughts he could create characters that make those of other novelists seem like dummies. And then he could tell how things *had* to happen. There is a current of necessity running through his books which helps to give them their infallible quality. Later novelists, who lacked his intuitive powers, were to think up more indirect and subtle ways of telling a story, but for Tolstoy there was only one way, which was the direct one, and only one truth, which was the one he saw, drawn in clear outlines and without ambiguity. It is because of this, because like God he could not describe any person or scene without pouring into them the breath of life, that he is by universal consent the greatest of all novelists.

‡ Gogol was a writer who came out of *Don Quixote* and *Tristram Shandy*. His short story, *The Nose*, is a splendidly extravagant development of Sterne's sort of humour. Then there is *The Overcoat*, from which all later Russian novels are said to be descended, and his brilliant and still frequently acted comedy, *The Inspector General*. But it is for his great novel, *Dead Souls*, that he chiefly lives today. The making of this is its plot, which was given him by Pushkin. The hero, or rather anti-hero, is a shady speculator in serfs who one fine morning arrives in his droshky in a small country town. After being taken up and fêted by the governor and the leading notables and thus initiated into all the tedium and banality of their small circle, he visits in turn five outrageously boring landowners and, as we form their acquaintance and plumb their different degrees of awfulness, we become aware that he is about to make them a very strange and delicate proposal – have they any recently dead serfs inscribed on their rolls whom they are willing to make over to him? We wait in expectation to see how they are going to react and are not disappointed. The book ends with a tremendous scandal that convulses the whole town and thus completes our knowledge of the baseness and ignominy of everyone in it. Incidentally it was from this scene that Dostoyevsky took the motif of rumour and scandal that he made such an important feature of his novels.

Gogol is one of the three or four supreme geniuses of the comic and his art, like that of all caricaturists, is based on a minute observation of apparently trivial details. It is an art of rich extravagance and buffoonery adding up to mordant satire, which he

derived both from his hatred of himself and from the difficulty
he found in adjusting to other people. He once said that all the
characters in *Dead Souls* came out of different sides of his own
personality. And what monstrosities they are! Never before have
dullness and insupportability been raised to such a sublime height.
There is something of the passion of Swift or Alfred Jarry in the
intensity of horror he felt for them and for the Russia they stood
for, so that we may say that he wrote *Dead Souls* to exorcise their
sinister and malignant qualities, their baseness and futility, and it
is this feeling, expressed with the greatest concentration and with
a mass of precise detail, that gives the book its potency. He called
it an epic poem and indeed in its rich and nuanced language, its
brilliant images and its exuberant wit and fantasy it rises above the
ordinary density of prose. The total effect is that of caricature, for
though, like Flaubert, Gogol was at heart a Romantic, lashing out
at the baseness of his age, his characters resemble those of Dickens
in their incapacity to develop (he said that he modelled his book
on Dante's *Inferno*, where life is over). Yet for all this the Russians
claim that his book contains more of the essence of their country
than that of any other writer. One reason for this may be that he
wrote it in Rome, whose medieval atmosphere he loved above
any other, and this gave him the perspective and contrast he
needed.

‡ Spanish literature stands out chiefly by its poetry, but it has also
produced two very great novels and one great novelist, not to
speak of an outstanding satirical writer, Quevedo. *La Celestina*, as
it is usually called, came out in 1499 and is thus the first novel to
appear in Europe. It is the story of two lovers, noble and well-born
and passionately in love, and around them there hovers a collection
of whores and pimps who are the go-betweens in their secret
meetings. The chief of these, the bawd Celestina, is one of the
most splendid and vivid characters in literature and her conversation and hedonistic philosophy fill the book and give it its
popular name. Thus, unlike *Romeo and Juliet*, it is not the lovers
who hold the centre of the stage, but the low-life characters who
have a greater interest for us because they are more endowed with
life and energy. In the end they all die violently, the lovers because
they are too obsessed by their passion and the others because in
their greed for money they overreach themselves. This plot sug-

gests a certain moral or philosophic attitude to life, but in fact it is the result of accident.

The other very great novel is of course *Don Quixote*, that masterpiece of ambiguity, which loses much of its subtlety in translation. The third novelist is Pérez Galdós. He could be called a pupil of Balzac, but he gains on him by knowing the world he writes about, which is Madrid from its beggars to its aristocrats, far better than Balzac knew Paris and the provinces. He writes with a Cervantean irony, which allows him many brilliant episodes, but his weakness is to be too prolix and in most cases to show little sense for form. For this reason his greatest and longest novel, *Fortunata y Jacinta*, has only just been translated.

‡ *Góngora*. This poet devised for his long poem *Las Soledades* a highly artificial system of metaphor and imagery, of the kind usually spoken of as precious, that seems to contradict every law of good writing in either verse or prose. It was also, till its key was rediscovered, almost totally impenetrable. For nearly three hundred years this poem was regarded as a monstrosity, whereas today it is generally recognized as being the greatest poem of any length in Spanish. I find it the one to which I return most often, for that is one of the effects which obscurity can produce. Critics of poetry too often forget that in this matter the proof of the pudding lies in the eating. The nature of the components and the method of preparation do not matter.

‡ As Eliot has said, every revolution in English poetry is apt to take the form of a return to common speech. But in Spanish poetry it appears as a return to popular or 'folk' poetry, which from the Middle Ages on had a very great influence because it was sung everywhere to a stringed accompaniment.

‡ Joyce's *Ulysses* is a supreme affirmation of life. No assemblage of people could be found who are more trivial, more squalid, more uninteresting than his characters and yet we are made to feel that they and their lives are somehow good – God's blessing on the world in Genesis. But the book requires in its readers the voracious, uncritical appetite of the young. Few adults can wade through

those nine hundred dense pages where, though there are a few linguistically beautiful passages and a wonderful end, they will hardly meet with one image or remark that quickens the pulse. *Ulysses* exists as literature through its starkness and directness of presentation and by its closeness to life, which completely break with the tradition of the past two thousand years. The apparently total passivity of the author before his material allows its scenes to come through without any intervention of the literary mind. In writing it Joyce drew on his two special gifts – a faculty of total recall of what is said and a musical ear which sometimes gives poetic form to the language.

It is in *Finnegans Wake* that one sees this latter gift carried furthest. There language breaks away from its normal function of communication and turns back upon itself. The medium becomes the object and words are linked together not so much by the syntax as through the interior echoes and puns. A new sort of poetry makes its appearance, but who has the patience to plough his way through it except in fragments? Evidently there can exist great works of literature which only a few fanatics can read.

‡ On re-reading Homer's *Iliad* in Richmond Lattimore's translation. Till this excellent verse translation appeared it was not possible to enjoy the *Iliad* unless one knew Greek. What a great poem! Yet I must say that I find many of the accounts of the fighting to be boring. There are too many of them for modern taste and they often suggest the reporting on the radio of a boxing match or bullfight instead of the tributes to the supposed ancestors of living families which in fact they were. It also seems strange to us that almost all the comic scenes should be laid among the gods, who often show themselves to be more prone to human weaknesses and less dignified and noble than are the warring heroes. We should be inclined to see a sceptical intention in this if we did not realize that the Greeks of this time were so filled with the notion of humanity that they had to make their gods as human as themselves. Homer's breadth and greatness come out best in the similes, which I imagine to be his personal contribution to the heroic lays that he took over from his predecessors. They not only display his warm humanity in the midst of such terrible scenes, but also his love of Nature and of everything in Nature. It is they that make this poem so life-enhancing. But the most

masterly thing in the *Iliad* is the plot. In this, their first poem that
has come down to us, the Greeks reveal what is their principal
contribution to European art and literature – their sense for
form.

The *Odyssey* is not such a great poem as the *Iliad*, though
perhaps more delightful to read. It suffers from being a mixture
of two different kinds of poems – an epic and an adventure story
that takes place in a fairy-tale setting. But it differs from all subsequent adventure stories, except perhaps Doughty's *Arabia Deserta*,
in that its hero is not seeking adventures but only wants to get
home to his wife and son. Dante's account in the *Inferno* of Ulysses'
last voyage is the fiction of a romantic age and very far in feeling
from the Greek spirit.

Writing

‡ It is by sitting down to write every morning that one becomes a writer. Those who do not do this remain amateurs.

‡ Self-conceit and shame are the occupational diseases of every writer. The stronger the self-conceit, the deeper the shame that follows, for who can look at the image of his own inadequacy as it is revealed in his work without flinching?

‡ 'I have the weakness of writing books and of being ashamed of them when I have written them' (Montesquieu (1689–1755), *Pensées et jugements*).

‡ Knowing what he has in him to give, how thwarting is the writer's realization that he has once again failed to provide it! Words are as recalcitrant as circus animals and the unskilled trainer can crack his whip at them in vain. Then, as Braque said, he has to learn to love the rule that corrects the emotion.

‡ The art of writing good prose or poetry lies in the art of correcting. This has to be painfully acquired. A poem is only finished when the poet can correct it no more.

‡ Correcting a prose manuscript is like something that happens to one when one is out hunting. Try as one may, one cannot hit on the appropriate phrase or image. That is, one's horse refuses

the fence. So one must ride him round the field, get him into a good mood, let him think that this fence is another fence and put him at it again.

‡ Writing rhymed verse is like taking part in an Alice-in-Wonderland steeplechase. As the horses gallop along they put up the fences they must jump over. If the fences are too low the poem is likely to be flat: if too high some of the horses will come a cropper. For the poem to be good nine out of the ten horses must finish well.

‡ Abstract painting is often the product of accidents. The painter finds in the run of the paint as he lays it on by brush or spray or dripping can certain configurations that suggest something meaningful to him. These he develops and works on till a painting that satisfies him gradually appears. Something like this can happen when a poet composes a poem. Unless he started off with a *vers donné*, he will have a general idea of what he wants to say, but as he goes along the words or images that rise up in his mind may lead him away from it, sometimes in a very different direction. The mere fact that a certain word comes for no apparent reason into his head and attracts him as much perhaps by its sound as by its meaning may affect the run of his verse. Thus in making a poem the poet needs to keep his mind in a very plastic state, holding on as much as possible to his original idea which will give the poem its general shape, but always on the lookout for the happy accident. For a poem, even more than a painting, lives, as Blake said, by its minute particulars.

‡ When I write a page that reads badly I know that it is myself who has written it. When it reads well it has come through from somewhere else.

‡ There is a mysterious power in every age which opens the gates for painters and writers in some directions and closes them in others. The most important faculty that any young writer can have is that of foreseeing when the red light is about to replace the green.

‡ A cow does not know how much milk it has until the milkman starts working on it. Then it looks round in surprise and sees the pail full to the brim. In the same way a writer has no idea how much he has to say till his pen draws it out of him. Thoughts will then appear on the paper that he is amazed to find that he possessed. 'How brilliant!' he says to himself. 'I had no idea I was so intelligent.' But the reader may not be so impressed.

‡ It is often as much what a writer leaves out as what he puts in that matters. Something must be left for the reader to add, for, as Valéry said, the writer provides one half and the reader the other.

‡ There is nothing so imprisoning to an experienced prose writer as a marked personal style. He should keep his pores and senses open and use any opportunity that offers for breaking out of his rut.

‡ To a writer or painter creation is the repayment of a debt. He suffers from a perpetual bad conscience until he has done this.

‡ Speaking with V. S. Pritchett of the writer's anxiety to finish his work before his death and his dread of that coming prematurely, we found ourselves in agreement. 'What is it we want?' I said. 'Not fame nor applause, nor even the sense of having succeeded. No, the impulse is simpler – we want to finish getting in the harvest we have been at so much trouble to sow.'

‡ *Ecstasy and inspiration.* In my hours of inspiration I am stronger than that hill, that person, that tree. In ecstasy they are stronger than me. When inspired I radiate out onto them and flatten them: in ecstasy they radiate onto me and I become one with them. The poet is a person who takes in passively for a long time, then gives out suddenly.

‡ Yeats said that we must choose between the perfection of the life and of the work. No doubt, but the quality of the work depends, among other things, upon the richness of the life. As

Bergson said, what we do depends on what we are. The writer and especially the poet should therefore direct his life so that he may become a deeper, more sensitive and more inwardly experienced person. Then he must plan his work so that it draws the best out of him.

‡ All serious novelists and poets write for posterity. This is because the only test of a work of literature is that it shall please other ages than its own.

‡ Philip II's confessors told him that in the next world he would be judged not on his personal life with its lecheries and adulteries, but on his acts as a king. So it is with writers. They are judged by their literary works and not by their moral conduct, though this will be reflected, sometimes in reverse, in their writings.

‡ George Fox, the Quaker, complained to the Lord that he was made to share the nature of Sodom and Egypt, of Pharaoh and Cain. 'And I cried on the Lord saying, "Why should I be thus, seeing that I was never addicted to commit these evils?" And the Lord answered that it was needful that I should have a sense of all conditions, else how should I speak of all conditions?'

‡ Every writer and artist wonders what in the world people of other professions can find to live for. This is the great advantage they possess, which more than makes up for the little they usually earn.

‡ Poets and painters are outside the class system, or rather they constitute a special class of their own, like the circus people and the gypsies. For the sake of their moral health they should be relatively poor and should mix mainly with their own kind. When they are short of money it is better for them to practise shop-lifting than to give lectures.

‡ All art, as Picasso said, is subversive. The writer's or painter's function is to work his way into the interstices of society and undermine it with his life-giving poisons. To Western society the artists are more dangerous than are the Marxists, whose aim is to make life twice as dead and conventional as it was before. And to Communist society they are more dangerous still, as the Soviet government well knows. Yet they should be tolerated, because like earthworms they turn over the soil and aerate it so that the trees and roses may grow. Nations that lack good poets and artists are like plains where saline deposits accumulate in a baked soil till nothing will grow there any longer.

‡ How writers are paid. Milton got £10 for *Paradise Lost*. Fifty years later Matthew Prior got 4,000 guineas for a collection of his verse.

‡ The complete writer puts all his enormous egotism into his books, so that if his best friend dies he resents having to give up his morning's work to go to his funeral.

‡ Illness or bad health can be a stimulus as well as a hindrance, as one may see in the cases of Keats and Baudelaire. But most writers have their worst illnesses not in their bodies but in their bank accounts. Anaemia, galloping consumption, wasting fever – the bank manager keeps them all in his files and to emphasize their severity inscribes them in red. These illnesses, when they are too prolonged, are the enemies of good literature.

‡ One night I dreamed that my way of starting a novel was all wrong and at once I began to dream of how I might do it better. A young man, at a loose end in life, goes to the theatre to see a play by Chekhov. Next to him in the stalls are two women, one of them perhaps thirty-five and the other a girl in her middle twenties. Both are attractive, but the older one especially so. They talk in the intervals and he hears snatches of their conversation which interest him.
At the end of the performance the two women go out and the

elder of them leaves her bag on the floor. He picks it up and
hurries after her to return it, but loses them in the crowd. So he
takes it home to his flat. On opening it he finds letters with a name
and address on them. He yields to the temptation to read them
and finds that they are love letters of a very passionate sort. On
the following day he calls at the address given on the envelope
and finds both the women at home. They press him to stay to
tea, the conversation goes well and he is invited to visit them
again. Gradually he gets drawn into their lives, but the question
– has he or has he not read the letters? – continues to perplex and
disturb the older woman. The dream went on a little, but this is
all I remember of it. I put it down as one of the many ideas for
books that have come down to me, but which have never got
written. So it is with all writers.

Ying Chü

‡ Ying Chü is a Chinese sage who lives in a cave in the province of Shansi, some two miles to the west of the town of Kolan. He is said to be a hundred years old and has so great a reputation for wisdom that eminent people from all over the world go to consult him. He was once rich and has travelled widely in Europe and Asia, but today he lives on the offerings of rice and vegetables that the peasants make him. Although he is not a Communist, Mao Tse-tung tolerated him and even from time to time asked his advice. Here are some of his answers to significant questions:

‡ H. G. Wells, during his stay at Peking, paid him a visit to ask what his opinion was on the Rights of Man. 'That is easily answered,' Ying replied. 'The rights of man are to have good health, as much money as one needs, a submissive wife who cooks well and attractive concubines. I might add an ear for music. If a man has all these he may expect, Heaven permitting, to enjoy a long and happy life.'

‡ The Archbishop of Canterbury, on a tour of Anglican missions, consulted Ying Chü on the question of whether the rich, notwith-standing the disparaging things that Jesus had said about them, could be saved. Ying replied, 'Confucius has said that the highest virtue a man can have is benevolence, and it is evident that the more money he possesses the more effective his benevolence will be.'

‡ When the French Minister for the Interior went to consult Ying Chü upon the best method of dealing with criminals, the sage said: 'A certain amount of violence in a country is a sign of health. It lets off steam and keeps people on their toes. So give your criminals a beating to teach them to respect the police and then let them go, but put in prison the householders and bank officials who allowed themselves to be robbed.'

‡ George Orwell visited Ying Chü to ask him whether he believed that all people were equal. 'They are equal,' he replied, 'in the sense in which all cows are equal, but some give more milk than others, and so are worth more.'

‡ Bertrand Russell on his visit to China sought out Ying Chü to ask him his opinion of Western philosophy. 'Most of your philosophizing,' he said, 'consists in trying to unravel the tangles that previous philosophers have made. Beating one's brains over such trivial matters is bad for the liver. Those who truly seek wisdom spend their days watching the river flow by and listening to the birds singing. Their nights they devote to love.'

‡ Hitler sent a secret emissary to Ying Chü to ask him whether or not he should invade Russia. Ying took a sip of tea before replying and then said – 'Why not?'

‡ Mr Heath, on his visit to China, went to ask Ying Chü's advice on how to deal with the large strikes that threatened the stability of the economy. 'A country,' Ying replied, 'that cannot be ruled by tradition and the right feelings of its inhabitants can only be ruled by force. My advice is that, if honest persuasion fails, you should send the union leaders and shop stewards for re-education to a labour camp and shoot the management to show that there is no class feeling. It is because Lenin and Stalin understood this that they have been the most successful rulers of this century.'

‡ Mr Wilson made a special visit to Ying Chü to consult him on the difficult problem of wage differentiation. Ying said, 'In every country the unintelligent outnumber the intelligent by five hundred to one. The latter ought therefore to be paid more, not because intelligence is intrinsically more valuable than its opposite, but because it is rarer. On the market gold fetches more than iron, though it is of less utility.'

‡ Lyndon Johnson sent an emissary to Ying Chü to ask him if he ought to continue the war for democracy in Vietnam or to withdraw from it. 'All strength,' replied Ying, 'both in armies and in nations is three parts bluff and window-dressing. You have put up a poor show in this affair and have lost much face, so that, if you continue to indulge yourselves in it, other nations will cease to fear you and you will end by losing all respect for yourselves. I advise you therefore to withdraw from it under some suitable pretext and make a landing on Mars instead.'

‡ Khrushchev sent a member of the Presidium to consult Ying Chü on whether or not the system of agricultural collectivization, which was giving such poor returns, should be scrapped and the land returned to the peasants, who worked it better. 'It is one of the inner contradictions of your creed,' replied Ying, 'that a choice has so often to be made between ideology, with its intellectually satisfying properties, and efficiency, with its merely materialistic ones. In the end you will have to decide whether you want your people to eat or not.'

‡ Mrs Thatcher made a special visit to China to ask Ying Chü whether, if British credit were to collapse, there was any likelihood that a Marxist revolution would break out. 'For your sake,' he replied, 'I fear not. A Marxist revolution in your country would give it a new life by reducing the population to a manageable size. In the long run that is the chief utility of these affairs. But unfortunately revolutions in highly industrialized states are no longer feasible. The ruling classes are too strong and well organized and the workers too prosperous to risk losing what they have. What you must expect for Britain is a gradual squeeze by which

it will be slowly pressed tighter and tighter together. It will be
the distinction of your country, to employ an astronomical simile,
to be the first of the White Dwarfs.'

‡ When Mr Nixon was last in China he took two days off to
visit Ying Chü. 'I am pleased to find you at home, Mr Chew,' he
said, shaking his hand warmly. 'Although I am a very busy man
I have come all this way to see you because I want to consult you
on what for me personally is a very important matter. That is –
does death end everything, or is there another life after this one?
I was brought up to believe that there is, but when I first went
to the White House I became infected by the tone of cynicism that
prevails in American politics and still more in the press, and so
I lost the innocent outlook of my early years and began to doubt.
Since I resigned from the Presidency this has worried me a lot.
I want – I particularly want – to live again because I feel that
I have been unjustly prevented from making a full use of my
talents in this life and that I have much yet to give. People tell
me, Mr Chew, that you are a well-informed person, especially
knowledgeable on these matters, and so I would like to ask you
your opinion on this. Can I hope to be reborn in another life and
fulfil my potentialities there?'
    'The desire to live again after death,' replied Ying Chü, 'is
very strong in some people. Worrying about it can have a bad
effect on the health. Whether or not we are reborn into another
existence, as the Buddhists believe, either as an ape or as a mouse
or as a prince or as a garbage collector, our well-being in this one
requires us to take things calmly and philosophically. However
I believe that I can offer you a way of getting over your trouble-
some obsession. You have only to consider that, if you are reborn,
you will not be the sole person to be so. Countless billions of men
and women will be reborn too, including all your compatriots,
some of whom you might prefer not to meet again. If then every
morning before you have breakfast you spend a few minutes
reflecting on this, I think I can promise that your craving for
immortality will leave you.'

‡ Asked by Mary McCarthy about the terrible crimes against
humanity that have been committed in recent years in Russia,

Germany and Vietnam, Ying Chü said: 'My latest information is
that God has realized that he has made a mistake. He chose the
wrong sort of ape from which to develop Man. Now, I gather, he
is considering whether he should not destroy everything and begin
over again.'

‡ At a scientific congress recently held at Lausanne to discover a
means of increasing the production of foodstuffs so as to meet the
needs of the rapidly mounting world population, it was decided
to send a deputation to China to consult the famous sage Ying
Chü. They found him seated at the mouth of his cave drinking tea
and, after bowing to him several times and enquiring about his
health, the head of the deputation put his question.

Ying Chü remained silent for some minutes before replying.
'This is a matter,' he said at length, 'that I have given much
thought to because it is especially important for my people. As
you know, during the past five thousand years all wars, emigrations
and colonizing enterprises have been caused by the lack of food
or raw materials in the home country. Today there are few empty
lands left that are suited for cultivation and the population of the
world is increasing by leaps and bounds. What then is to be done?
All things considered, the only effective solution would seem to
lie in the adoption of anthropophagy or cannibalism, which would
not only provide food in the form of a good protein diet, but
reduce progressively the number of mouths to be fed. Up to the
present a strong but irrational inhibition has prevented men from
considering this, but as the emergency becomes more pressing this
prejudice is likely to weaken, so that we may expect before long
to see a far-sighted ruler appear on the scene who will organize
this procedure scientifically on utilitarian principles. We human
beings are an adaptable race, so I see no reason to doubt that,
with the help of a well-conceived propaganda service, we shall
overcome our prejudices as soon as necessity stares us in the face.
Human flesh is said to be delicious, which suggests that, after
an initial repulsion, the taste for it will grow. For the squeamish
it could be converted into a pâté. By choosing the right specimens
for our consumption – proceeding, that is to say, on strictly
eugenic lines – we could weed out the physically weak and the
ideologically unaccommodating and so in time improve the quality
of our race. That would be more positively constructive than

eliminating the ruling classes, who generally speaking are the
cream of the population. We should also be less apt to indulge
in the sin of eating animals, who are often, as is well known, our
ancestors in disguise.

'It may of course be objected that such a practice is contrary to
custom and therefore immoral. But against that we can put Marx's
well-known dictum that ethical values are not built into human
society but are manifestations of some phase of the historical
process. Whatever benefits the masses must be good because the
age is on their side. And anyhow who are we to object? Have we
not in the course of the past sixty years learned to kill off in cold
blood some fifty millions of our kind, mostly for no particular
reason? Surely, that being our nature, it would seem a mere
caprice if in a great extremity we could not eat them as well. Indeed
by doing so we would be giving a rational sanction to our destructive
propensities by putting their cadavers to a sensible and humane
use. If this proposal jars on you I would ask you to consider it
more carefully at your leisure, because for my part I cannot see
how any person who claims to be rational can dissent from it,
though I agree that, men's prejudices being what they are, we
must give the idea time to grow and mature.'

The delegation thanked Ying Chü and left. Its more broad-
minded and liberal members thought that, since the proposal was
obviously based on reason, it ought to be carefully considered,
whereas its Communist members were deeply shocked, saying
that Marx had only said that the bourgeoisie should be destroyed,
not eaten as well.

People

FROM A NOVELIST'S NOTEBOOK

‡ *Bores.* Treat them kindly, for they are Ancient Mariners, purging their sins by painful penance. One day these sins will drop off them, their boringness will cease and they will float up to heaven out of sheer gaiety of spirit with all the dross of their obsessions washed away.

‡ He thought that because he had freckles and sandy hair and a trim moustache he was more *real* than other people. If he lacked good looks and intelligence he had this compensation. On it he based his confidence in life, and since self-confidence is the secret of success, he succeeded both in his love-affairs and in his business.

‡ Dressing took him a long time because as he washed and shaved he was the Prime Minister making a speech on foreign affairs.

‡ Some men hate their sons because they are jealous of their wife's love for them. This is the Laius complex, which sets up in the son an Oedipus complex. But it often happens that men who have reached a certain eminence in life or who are proud of their own talents hate and despise their sons because they do not come up to the standard to be expected in sons of such a remarkable father.

‡ He sometimes hated his friends for the same reason that elderly women hate looking-glasses. They made him display his weaknesses.

‡ He had not so much a life instinct as a show-off instinct. That is to say, everything he did well lost its value because he boasted of it.

‡ Some people feel they do not exist unless they are being noticed. For them *esse est percipi*.

‡ He was a man who liked his friends, yet whenever one of them was mentioned he said something disparaging about him.

‡ He flattered people as a way of keeping them at a distance. Or was it that he wanted to show his superiority by patronizing them?

‡ A lady he had the feeling of having met before came up to him in the street. 'I'm sorry,' he said. 'I know your name but I'm bad at remembering faces.'

‡ Through inattention he began to smile on being told that her husband was suffering from a painful disease.

‡ People could poison their wives or their husbands, cheat at cards, commit incest with their mothers or join the Plymouth Brethren or the Trotskyist Party, and he didn't care. He only objected to visitors who stayed too long.

‡ Some people suffer from a self-defeating mechanism. Their aggressiveness of manner is often a sign of their wanting to be liked. 'How dare you not like me?'

‡ He was a terrible arguer, but he did not argue with real people but with dummies which he set up in their place. 'You think that...' he would say, though his friend thought something quite different.

‡ He was an enormous egotist. How was it then that he had caught such an attractive girl? Was it because he enfolded her in his own egotism and spoke for both? Certainly she had never been so drawn out and flattered before.

‡ Marion prided herself on having no illusions. She believed that she could see through everything and everyone and read the hidden truth beneath. She was so sure of herself that one trusted her. And then suddenly she would say, 'Of course you know that the BBC is staffed entirely by Communists.'

‡ 'Why can't he be himself?' one says of people who put on an act. Yet it may be that 'himself' is just what one wouldn't want him to be.

‡ How is it that, when we meet with a certain person, we know at once that there are a thousand others exactly like him? Some particulars dress as universals.

‡ When he repeated a conversation he had had with another person, it was always his own words that he remembered best. 'So I said to Picasso...'

‡ As a municipal counsellor M. found that there was a great advantage in having a reputation for strict honesty. Whenever he was approached over a building contract he was offered a larger bribe.

‡ A mild-mannered man, he was given to fits of impatience, boiling over like milk at a low temperature. A moment later he had forgotten it, but his wife remembered, for he had humiliated her in public.

‡ The rich do not understand our problems. On hearing that a friend of his was in trouble, a wealthy industrialist asked, 'Is it *just* a question of money?'

‡ His name was Marmaduke Stinker. When his young wife suggested to him that he should change it by deed poll, he replied that he could not do that because it went back to Tudor times. Thirteen Stinker ancestors in direct succession were not a thing to be sniffed at, especially as one of them had been a general. However, he went on, the word had originally been written with a 'y' and in these democratic times, when birth and lineage were disparaged, it might be well for him to assert himself and revert to the old spelling.

‡ She was so busy protecting herself against any possible hint of reproach that she could not wait to take in what was said to her. Her replies therefore operated on a hair-trigger.

‡ She envied everyone their diseases. No one could say that they had had an illness without her claiming to have had a worse one herself.

‡ She was continually struck by the guilt to be seen in the faces of the old. They were guilty because they were old. Did this mean, in the case of the men, too old to make love to her?

‡ There are women whose bodies are so sensuously developed that one knows at first sight that all their thoughts and perceptions must filter through them.

‡ She had one of those empty smiles that seemed designed to lubricate the words she was using and make them go down well.

‡ She had large eyes of a vaguely dark colour that seemed intended more for expressing feelings of a dolorous sort than for seeing with.

‡ Her whole life was governed by her desire not to be blamed, so she never did anything and got blamed for that.

‡ A woman cried for an hour at the death of her daily help's child, whom she scarcely knew, but did not drop a tear at the death of her oldest friend, which she heard of in a letter. Crying is infectious, like sneezing.

‡ An elderly, very pious Quakeress. The instincts that had been elsewhere repressed showed themselves in an excessive development of the mouth and lips. She did not allow herself to eat much, but when she took something she liked she made a smacking sound as she ate it.

‡ A certain woman who was no longer young but still retained much of her beauty took to dressing in old frumpy clothes that did not suit her. This was a test. Would her charm and beauty come through in spite of them? Her pride required that she give them hurdles to leap over.

‡ She was intelligent and perceptive and had a fine taste in the arts, but she was inarticulate. She could not explain her point of view on anything. This made her arrogant and dogmatic in intelligent company. *She* knew and they didn't, and it maddened her that she could not convince them that this was the case.

‡ There are women who develop a perverse streak out of an instinct of flirtatiousness. They contradict their lovers and advance absurd opinions because they feel that it raises their value. A little of this in an attractive woman can enhance her charm, because some men like to equate femininity with irrationality, but too much of it will make her tedious.

‡ Women often reveal the idea they have of themselves in their dress. That preposterous pink hat, that mauve frilled blouse on the elderly lady at the corner table betrays to all the world the romantic picture she has of herself. That purple cloak on the lady literature don is an assertion that she is a bohemian at heart. Once, these garments are saying, I was the belle of the ball, once I lived with the poets in Paris, and I have not changed. This is me. How ridiculous we should all of us look if we had not learned to conceal our secret estimation of ourselves!

‡ On weekends at the A.s' house they often play a certain game. A shipwreck is imagined, the ship is going down and there is a rush for the boats. How will their absent friends behave in such a situation? All agree that Matthew will find himself in the first boat – the one that is reserved for the women – without having been seen to get into it, while Stephen will go down with the ship out of an excess of nobility.

‡ One winter evening Sir Leo Chiozza Money, a public figure of the twenties, was discovered by the police in a compromising situation with a prostitute in Hyde Park. He was arrested and charged with indecency in public. Winston Churchill's comment was: '*Five* degrees of frost! *seventy* years of age! It makes me proud to be an Englishman.'

‡ 'My aunt Brooking was a turbulent woman in temper; noe such way as pleasing her; always bad. She was never sick, did eat but little at table, and filled her body in a closet. Would run out against extravagances and her neighbours' way of living. A true Englishwoman. Played the devill at home and a deverting, afabill woman abroad. Beloved out of doors, but a devill in.' (*Rambling Jack*, an autobiography by R. Raynall Bellamy (1700–1770), published by Jonathan Cape in 1936)

Nature

‡ To believe, as most biologists seem to, that the huge variety of living species, each of them of a fantastic complexity, has developed solely through the operation of natural selection working on chance mutations, demands a faith in the miraculous that I for one am not prepared to give. Since most mutations are harmful, the time required for this to happen must approximate to the time required by a troop of monkeys playing with typewriters to produce the text of *Hamlet*. If most of our biologists were not so obsessed by mechanical explanations they would see that there must be some other factor at work besides chance and necessity. Since living creatures have their mental as well as their physical aspect and science is tied to the physical, the processes of life remain a mystery.

‡ Behind the scientific theory lies the scientist's presuppositions. He wants to understand life, so for a model he takes machines which he understands because he made them. Yet not everything in evolution can be explained in this way. How, for example, can certain complex forms or organs such as the eye or the speech organs, which are useless unless they are complete and fully developed, make their appearance in a living creature unless there is something in the life process that we can call a sense of direction or purpose? Yet any theory that may be offered to account for this is likely to be misleading, for we are moving at the limits of thought and language. We cannot trace back in time the mental element or aspect that seems always to accompany the physical because it leaves no traces. All we can do is to admit our ignorance.

‡ *Wonders of evolution.* When an owl is hunting for mice over a field it hoots. This warns the mice to freeze so that they will not be seen or caught. If it did not hoot it would soon catch all the mice and then starve, so its hooting benefits both itself and the mice. To take another instance, an antelope's scent tells the lion it is not far away and in a certain direction and this helps to keep the number of these animals down so that they do not overstock their pasture lands. How can we explain this interaction of factors in wild life which preserves the balance of Nature except by saying that evolution operates as a single whole and on a broad front?

‡ Why should biologists always assume that every feature or organ that a plant or animal possesses should have been retained because it is an advantage to it? It is the fox's powerful scent that gives it away, the peacock's tail that delivers it to its enemies. May it not possess organs that, if not actually harmful like the appendix, are neutral and can even, when passed on in the course of time to other species and modified by them, acquire a utility? We do not, I suspect, yet understood all the ways in which evolution operates.

‡ We imagine that we are many times more intelligent than the birds and animals and in most senses that is true. But the greater part of our intelligence is due to the fact that we have learned to speak a language which enables us to communicate not only our feelings and intentions, as they also can, but concrete facts and experiences and to elaborate them by means of concepts. We did not learn to do this because we were so much more intelligent than our cousins the apes, the dolphins and the elephants, but because we happened at just the right moment to develop the necessary vocal organs. Since then our intelligence has grown by leaps and bounds because speech and its later consolidation in writing have drawn it out and developed it. The medium took hold of us and carried us along towards new horizons and new achievements. Yet in this process we have also lost something, because speech and writing deform our feelings and perceptions. Words are symbols representing experiences, so that by thinking in them we lose that immediate sensual contact with the world around us which animals and young children possess. To speak,

we have to select and analyse – that is, break up and mutilate – the continuous web of our experience, and thus there is a loss of sensitivity and awareness. So, since our written language draws us more and more every year in the direction of the abstract, it has become the task of our poetry and painting to move in the opposite direction and to take us back to that primitive Eden which we were driven out of long ago – the Eden of immediate sensual contact with Nature. We need both to move forward in our pursuit of conceptual elaboration and discovery – that is, in science – and back to our roots in that untutored life of the senses where we are at one with the plants and animals. This should be for us the meaning of Nature. The human world of today is too penned in, too parochial: we need to look out from time to time like seals from their breathing holes in the ice and see ourselves as the end-product of a long process that goes back to the amoeba. For us, in our occasional moments, the fierceness of the tiger, the terror of the antelope which is also its delight in its swiftness, the freedom of the bird to pierce the air, the sensuality of the snail hidden in its moist couch of leaves, the ecstasy of the poplar tree waving its branches in the wind. It is only by this sympathy with every stage of our biological past that we can recover our lost heritage.

‡ Every animal and bird is a specialist which takes in and masters all the minutiae of its environment that bear on either its need for food or for mating, and shows little or no interest in anything else. Most animals during a large part of the year lead obsessed and harassed lives, driven by fear and menaced by enemies, though in their rare moments of repletion they can luxuriate in a sense of well-being and display their high spirits and their delight in their own skill. Very few birds or animals expect to eat regularly or to reach middle age, yet we should not pity them too much, for it is the spur of hunger and danger that keeps them alert and well. Man is the only animal that suffers from boredom, because his life is artificial.

‡ Flying acts on birds as a liberating sublimation. It is through this that they have learned to express their feelings about love and about the acquisition of a territory for breeding in through ritual

dance and song. Their discovery of flying and the sense of leisure and delight it gives them is what makes birds closer to us in our aesthetic feelings, whereas the animals are closer to us in the moral and practical life.

‡ Birds live on a more rapid time-scale than we do and have sharper eyesight, and their nervous reactions are quicker and their body temperature higher. They have also an elaborate system of communication that we are only beginning to get some idea of through slow-motion films and sound recordings. Their courtship rituals can be extremely complex and proceed not only by songs (which often contain sub-songs) but by graduated movements or gestures, yet what is conveyed is rather a mood or an emotion than a piece of information. We also, as all lovers know, possess some of these unconscious modes of communication, but as a rule much less completely than the birds or animals. Thus it can happen that a dog understands its master's frame of mind better than his wife does. But young children possess them too and a baby will react to small changes in its mother's feelings of which she is hardly aware. A medium or thought-reader is a person who is endowed with some of this primitive sensitivity which education and the coarse contacts of daily life tend to overlay.

‡ 'The cuckoo is a pretty bird – it sings as it flies...' (from a song collected near Asheville in the Appalachians from a hillbilly who had never seen a cuckoo and could not read).

The cuckoo is an orphan whose call or song is simple because it has not learned it from its parents. It is a very restless bird, for if it stays too long in one place it is mobbed by small birds who take it for a hawk. No other problems trouble it, for it lives on the hairy caterpillars that it finds on the leaves of trees and which other birds will not eat because their taste is so disgusting. It is a solitary bird, without family ties, that delights in its own freedom, and its call is designed to challenge other males as much as to attract a female. Thus when she appears with her low bubbling note he does not remain with her for more than a minute or two, but is off again at once. The female is as solitary as the male, only more shy and retiring. Like him she is promiscuous and allows all the males in the district to copulate with her, so that his challenge to them must be more a formality than a mark of possessiveness and jealousy. She lays her small eggs on the ground and, as everyone knows, carries them in her beak to the nest of a hedgesparrow or warbler, which receives them unwillingly but ends by accepting them. When the young bird is hatched it pushes its foster-brothers out of the nest and their mother makes the best of a bad job and continues to feed it. This lack of responsibility in the female cuckoo for her young has been severely commented on by ornithologists, but it would seem that she has her reasons. In the West Indies there is a cuckoo, *Cuculus ani*, that builds a large, rough nest and sits in it in the company of several other females of the same species. They hatch out their chicks together. Can it be that the female cuckoos of Europe have adopted their unmaternal habits because they are bored by a solitary incubation in which they get no help or encouragement from their restless, bachelor mates?

‡ Professor W. H. Thorpe in his admirable book *Animal Nature and Human Nature* (1974) tells us that the hump-backed whale sings a song containing some 200 notes which is exactly the same in its musical notation as that of the wren, except that it lasts for ten minutes whereas that of the wren lasts for only three seconds. It sings at a depth of between 1,000 and 2,500 feet below the surface of the sea and its song can be heard by other whales at a distance of between 2,000 and 3,000 miles. We are exterminating these whales as fast as we can for products that can be almost as easily obtained synthetically.

‡ The wren, *Troglodytes troglodytes*, is the smallest of European birds and perhaps the most popular, for it has a large folklore attached to it and in France is known by 140 different vernacular names. By a very ancient tradition it was regarded as the king of the birds, as its German name *Zaunkönig*, or King of the hedgerows, and its Swedish name *Kungsfägel*, or Kingbird, show. And in a mythological sense it was a very real king, for though normally it was held to be a crime to injure it or take its eggs, on one day in every year, just before or after Christmas, it was hunted and killed and its body carried round the village on a pole decorated with leaves, sometimes by torchlight with fifes playing, and buried

in state in the churchyard after being blessed by the priest. In some parts of southern Europe the man who killed it was treated as a king, dressed in royal robes, given a crown and sceptre and feasted that night at the public expense. This shows that the ceremony goes back to prehistoric times when sacred kings were elected at the beginning of every year and sacrificed at the end of it. This 'hunting of the wren', as it was called, continued to be observed in a watered-down form, as a means of obtaining pennies for little boys, in some English villages to the beginning of this century. It took place on St Stephen's Day, now better known as Boxing Day.

The wren of the ornithologists is a tiny, rather plump brown bird with a short cocked-up tail, very lively and inquisitive, which spends its days hunting for insects among dead leaves at the bottom of a hedge, where it is easily taken for a mouse. It is found all over Europe as far as the Arctic Circle, and it must be due to its extraordinary vitality that it stands the cold winters so well. It has a sweet, piercing, very rapid little song, less resigned than that of the hedge-sparrow and, as I have said, having the same musical notation as that of the whale. It builds a large domed nest in bushes, or rather two domed nests, one of which is never occupied. This is said to be built by the male in competition with its mate, but since it is she who lays the eggs it is always her own nest that she chooses. As a boy I several times found these empty nests, but since both sexes look exactly alike it would be difficult to confirm the truth of their origin.

‡ One of the most beautiful and endearing of all birds is the bee-eater, which is a summer visitor to the Mediterranean region. It has the brilliant blue, red and yellow plumage of the kingfisher, ending in a long green tail, and the swift, gliding flight of the swallow. It is also provided with a long beak with which it digs a tunnel in sand cliffs in which to lay its five white eggs. Bee-eaters nest in colonies and are one of the most talkative of birds, for as they swoop and dive in pursuit of the bees and wasps they feed on, they keep up a lively, chuckling conversation. They are not afraid of human beings and will nest within a few yards of a house, but the most usual place to come on them is perched on telegraph wires by the roadside or flying around near-by in circles. One can say that they are the characteristic bird of southern Spain, as

noticeable and far more numerous than rooks are in England, but in August, when the bees stay in their hives because there are no more flowers for them to visit, they set off to cross the Sahara, travelling by night and resting in the oases, to winter in the forests and parklands of equatorial Africa. In the following April they return to their old nesting sites in Europe.

‡ The snail, that charming inhabitant of damp corners, which has the honour of having had a folksong addressed to it, is the pest of gardeners but the friend of children. It is a hermaphrodite and can copulate simultaneously with both sexes. It is also a cupid, for to stimulate its prospective mate it will shoot at it a tiny four-fluted crystalline dart which it keeps in a quiver next to the glands on its female duct. The maximum range of its shot is two and a half inches. It has other curious habits. Its eyes are on the ends of its horns and when it has indigestion it can put one of them down its gullet to see what the trouble is. Then, as everyone knows, when it has to cross a rough patch of ground, it lays down a carpet of slime from a gland in its foot to make the passage smoother. Every child should keep a snail farm of different species and make them run races.

‡ Not far from the snail but more deeply hidden away one will find the toad, *Bufo vulgaris* (or if one is lucky its loud-croaking cousin *Bufo calamita*, the natterjack) with its livid warty skin and its beautiful ruby-red eyes. It is the prince in disguise whom the girl of the fairy tale took into her bed and by so doing released from its enchantment. Every garden has one and, since it seeks the dark, its usual habitat is a corner in the potting shed. What touches me about this animal is its total incapacity for defending itself. It cannot hop like a frog, it can only crawl slowly and painfully on legs that are too weak to support it, and its mouth has no teeth to bite with. The only defence it has lies in its strange, uncanny appearance and in its perfect immobility, which will usually keep a cat or a dog at arm's length. A toad is also an indispensable pet or familiar for a witch and I remember around 1930 a Dorset woman saying to me of a certain wrinkled old crone, 'Oh *she*! She is the sort that keeps a toad in a drawer.'

‡ I kneel down and peer into the long grass of a field and watch the insects moving about. Ants run from stalk to stalk, great beetles brush past like long-distance buses, little beetles scurry by, ladybirds climb up the tall stems and then descend again. Insects of many kinds pass and repass and all without greeting one another, without taking notice of one another, without chasing or devouring one another. They seem to be completely absorbed in their own concerns, seeing nothing round them, always in a hurry, making their way like businessmen in a crowded street to some unknown destination. The beauty of this forest of grass stems and leaves that they are travelling in is evidently lost on them: they see in it only obstacles that have to be laboriously circumvented and remain fixed like automatons in their obsession. This is surely a very different world to ours, a world as remote and impenetrable to our minds as would be that of the inhabitants of another planet. To learn anything about it one must open a book on insects written by some infinitely patient entomologist and then one will be amazed at the complexity of their lives and habits.

‡ Nature has shown herself at her most inventive in her creation of insects. She may well be proud of this, for they were her first experiment in advanced forms of life, launched some two hundred million years ago, and have in many respects turned out to be her most successful. The proof of this is that there are at least a million different species of them in the world today and that most of these have been very little modified since their first appearance, whereas the reptiles, birds, marsupials and mammals have undergone continual transformations as well as many catastrophic failures and bankruptcies. The chief reason for this seems to be that they have been endowed with highly developed patterns of behaviour, whether social or individual, which have come to them ready-made through their genes. No cerebration for them: all or almost all of their operations are automatic. Nature has not merely thrown them into life but has kept a strict control over their actions, whereas when she made man she put a wide power of choice into his hands and thus took a risk that, since it has led to the creation of the atom bomb, may prove to be disastrous.

Then she has shown an amazing ingenuity in the construction of their bodies. What chiefly differentiates insects from reptiles, birds and mammals is that they have no internal skeleton, but instead a hard external coating of a substance called chitin that holds their frames together. This limits their size and with that their brains so that Nature has to do most of their thinking for them. It also sets a difficult problem. Since this cuticle or exo-skeleton, as it is called, encloses their bodies in a tight case which cannot expand as they grow, it has to be shed from time to time, a procedure that is all the more exacting because it extends into the digestive canal and through the air-tubes that carry oxygen to the tissues. This makes it a dangerous operation which requires the insect to lie low for a period both before and after, and often leads to its death or to the loss of a limb. It is the need for providing with reasonable safety for this periodic change that has led to the process known as metamorphosis by which an insect goes through several life-stages such as, in the case of the lepidoptera, egg, cater-pillar, chrysalis and butterfly or, in that of the dragonfly, egg, larva, nymph and imago – that is, sexually mature insect. A pro-digious number of variations of this pattern have been evolved in the course of ages, together with an equally prodigious diversity in the bodily structures and modes of living. In all the smaller forms of life Nature has shown a marked inventiveness and love of complexity, whereas, when she tried her hand at reptiles and mammals, she introduced a great simplification.

‡ Nearly all insects have wings so that they may lay their eggs where the larvae will find something to eat, forage for themselves and spread their species. The exception to this is the spider, which has a device that is very much better, its silk threads. Thus anyone who goes out to a bushy place on a fine autumn morning will see spiders launching themselves out on these threads like balloonists. If the breeze is strong they may be carried for several miles, and this gives them such a good opportunity for disseminating their species that if it were not for another ingredient in their nature they would be much more numerous than they are. This is their propensity to cannibalism. The female spider, as is well known, is much larger than the male and after copulating with him, she eats him or, if she does not happen to be hungry at the moment, she ties him up to eat later. She also eats her young and they will eat one another if wet weather keeps them from migrating, so that in this way their numbers are greatly reduced. No doubt we must see in this a wise provision of Nature for ensuring that the population

of this too successful insect is kept within the limits that its food supply will allow. As it is, many house spiders have to go for weeks without a bite.

‡ We owe to insects the pleasure we get from the colours of flowers as well as their perfume. They are the advertisement hoardings the plants put out to draw the insects to their corollas by the promise of nectar because in the course of getting it they will act as intermediaries in their sexual relations and so fertilize them. The colour they most delight in is ultraviolet, which we cannot see because our range in the spectrum does not include it, whereas their range nearly always excludes red. So if poppies are popular with bees and other insects, that is because, besides the red we see, they also reflect ultraviolet. But sometimes flowers attract insects by the direct promise of sex. Thus the flowers of the *Ophrys* genus, which is a member of the Orchid family, provide close imitations of bumble-bees, wasps, spiders and various sorts of flies. The males of these insects hatch out a week before the females and, looking round for a mate, see the flowers of these orchids and endeavour to copulate with them. Then the females hatch out and the insects desert their floral loves.

Bees and most other insects are sensitive to form as well as to colour. They cannot distinguish between squares, triangles and circles, but are very aware of the differences in spiral or whorl-shaped forms such as flower petals display. This shows how close is the interdependence of flowering plants and insects: both appeared at the same time in the Mesozoic age and grew up in close association with one another.

‡ Except when it produces crystals, Nature abhors straight lines. Its forms are circles, cylinders, tubes, ovals, spirals and curved surfaces of every sort. But men, birds and insects naturally think in straight lines, for these are the lines followed by light.

‡ Man is the only animal to make war, if one excludes hyaenas, who form into small gangs to raid and to defend their territory. But among the insects there are some species of ant that have taken to warfare as a profession. They raid other ant-hills, massacre

the population, carry away the food they find stored and also the larvae, which they bring up as slaves to work for them. Many ancient peoples have lived in this way, beginning with the Assyrians. Today we deprecate war and favour revolution instead, but in past times war has been of great value in promoting civilization. It has supplied the wealth and the slaves that advanced cultures required if they were to develop those superior techniques that have led to our present eminence. And recent wars at least have had a liberating effect which has helped to raise the living standard of the working population. But in aggressiveness *à l'outrance* we are left behind by certain species of insects. An example of this is the bulldog ant of Australia, which seems to have fighting and killing in its genes. If one of them is cut in two a battle begins between the head and the tail. The head seizes the tail with its teeth and the tail defends itself by stinging the head. The battle may last for half an hour till either they die or are dragged apart by other ants. One is reminded of Ulster.

‡   The wild deer, wandering here and there,
        Keeps the human soul from care.
        (Blake)

But not, it would seem, the kangaroos. According to Alan Moorehead the Australians are killing a million of them every year for pet-food. The British are performing a million operations a year on animals without anaesthetics. The Americans are exterminating the rhesus monkeys of India, many of them dying in transit through overcrowding. In Bengal only one tiger remains of the fifty that roamed the jungles not long ago. The whales are being rapidly killed off. The Turks are massacring the dolphins. In Britain the domestic animals are being kept in farm factories under brutal and degrading conditions. Our songbirds are being netted, trapped and shot in enormous numbers (160 million last year) as they pass through Italy. Two million Italians come out with their guns on Sundays and are free to shoot on any land that they please. All this in an age that boasts of its love for animals.

‡ Great Pan is dead. The nymphs of the woods and streams have departed and the electric generators have taken their place. But

some of our psychic roots, which attached us to life, have gone with them and so we say, as none of our ancestors would have said, that life is pointless and absurd.

‡ When we are happy we love Nature. When we are dull and depressed it says nothing to us. Our feeling for it would therefore seem to be a reflection of our moods. But if we examine with a magnifying glass the structure of flowers and leaves we will find a beauty of contrivance and symmetry that is quite independent of our moods and feelings. This is the true beauty of Nature, inherent in its particular forms, but it does not act upon us as powerfully as landscape, which is a looking-glass we hold up to our states of mind.

‡ 'He thought the stars as fair now as when they were in Eden, the sun as bright, the sea as pure' (Thomas Traherne, *Centuries of Meditation*).

‡ 'The colours of the grove and the voice of the birds will bestow immortality' (Jalal'uddin Rumi).

‡ The rawness of Nature, of its perfumes, its stars, its rustling trees, the intractable quality of its beauty so untranslatable into human symbols, opened before me, broke upon me suddenly with a kind of pain. What could *I* do with all this? What equivalent could human life provide for the ferocity of outward things? All this was, as Jules Laforgue said, 'too far from my village'. (Yegen, 1923)

‡ Every voice in Nature is a human voice.

‡ 'The Christians and the Gnostics think it proper to call violent men their brothers, but refuse to speak thus of the sun or of the stars; and with insane mouth separate the soul of the world from an alliance with ours' (Plotinus, *Enneads*). Christianity, following

Judaism, broke the link between Man and Nature which the Greeks
had held to be divine.

‡   *Blackbird singing*

The light was quiet and the sun had set.
   The garden was quiet too, cherubic rose
the clouds that seemed to be fish. Their rosy tint
   drove back the darkened trees into a vase
from which the blackness bellied like a net.
   The light was quiet for the sun had set.

The evening became itself, a zigzag flight
   between the bright and the dark, the near and the far,
the cresting wave above and the prostrate beach,
   and then a sound began to explore the air,
sewing the earth and sky into one cloth.
   The evening became itself, the flick of a bat.

The singer knew his task. He taught the night
   the words the day had muttered, taught the day
the music that other days had locked in night.
   He taught the past to the present, the then to the now
and what he sang came to his throat untaught.
   The singer knew his task. His words were right.

The song had been well rehearsed. Ages before
   a blackbird singing at dusk had cast a spell
over a hermit rapt in heaven-seeking prayer
   under a hazel tree beside his cell.
When the monk woke five centuries had passed.
   The far had become the near, the near the far.

So, voice in the garden, sing for me again.
   Take me from time, raise me to different light
where the past and the present merge into one thing
   where the Always is always Itself and the air is bright.
Teach me to glimpse the invisible sunshine
   where the Many is also the One and the pattern
   complete.

(1957)

‡ A fine flower, a tall tree – these are so miraculous in their complexity and beauty that we would like to be able to spend the whole day looking at them. Yet our attention flags at the end of a moment. Is this because they live on a different time-scale from us? For if we see a speeded-up film of them we can be enthralled by the drama of their growth and development, since nowhere is the struggle for existence more tense than in the vegetable world. Yet normally we see them as examples of perfect attainment and fulfilment in a slower-moving sphere than our own, and it is for that reason that we both desire them and cannot stay with them. Our nature hurries us on.

‡ On looking at a winter hedgerow full of grass and nettles after some months spent in London, to recapture through them odd moments of one's past life, not in themselves remarkable, when the attention was occupied by nothing in particular. There is a strange pleasure in recovering the actual feel of a past experience, even if it was dull and insignificant. For the past is that part of us which is gone for ever. (1925)

‡ The charm of the English countryside with its fields and hedges lies in the rediscovery of things known long ago and familiar since childhood. That of foreign countries lies in their unfamiliarity. (1922)

‡ *Notes on the great freeze* (January 1940; from a diary). I had cycled over from Aldbourne to Maiden Court to have tea and supper with V. S. and Dorothy Pritchett. Coming back at midnight I felt frozen from the waist downwards and boiling hot above as I drove my bike up the hills. The stars looked down in fury, red and green and blue. I felt like an engine driver at a junction, looking out for signals I did not understand. Yes, the stars were angry with us, I said to myself, because we did not follow their instructions. Hence wars, famines, plagues, calves born with two heads and children with gills instead of mouths. Big birds like vultures, their feathers puffed out with the cold, stood inert in the hedges.

Next morning the panes of the windows were covered with

frost etchings. One was a scene of the Crystal Palace fireworks, another a mountain with pine trees on it, another Wellington saying 'Up, boys, and at'em.' After breakfast we cycled to Great Bedwyn with the idea of skating on the canal. A dense purple cloud like a feather mattress bulged from the sky and opened. The snow flew out, carried by a violent wind. It was a pretty sight as the little village with its railway station, canal and church, like one of those model villages from which one learns German in a school reading book, was suddenly covered by a slanting fall of snow.

That night the moon looked like a spider in the centre of its web. It destroyed the force of gravity in the landscape, extending the feeling for space. The hills were like light mantles. Walking down a lane between soft white foliage, the cold fell on us from the sky.

By day steaming pond and stream. The frozen trees, bearing clusters of thrushes and blackbirds puffed out by the cold and waiting to be fed. Others circling to keep warm or dying and lying stiff by the roadsides. Cycling downhill was like being a diamond cutting a pane of glass. The village under a light coat of snow looked like a wedding cake in a shop window with the icing a little worn off.

‡ These are the flowers that come out in my garden in May: tulips with their long stalks and their debutante air; lilac with its memory-laden smell; anemones with their naked colours; columbines with their frilled cotton dresses; peonies with their Titianesque richness of colour; scillas with their blue of an inlet in the sea; alkanet and borage, a deeper blue in liqueur glasses; pansies with their velvet faces; thyme and aubrietia, *bouches béantes* in the sun.

In June come the strong perfumes. Roses first, the best of them 'General Jacqueminot', 'Gloire de Dijon' and the moss roses; pinks, warm and intimate; box hedges that smell of walled gardens; tobacco plants, Englishly exotic like the cry of the owl and the nightjar; stocks, fine threads of Grasse perfume; mignonettes, subtle; poppies, sultry; the herbs, homely; honeysuckle, the sweetness of English lanes; *Lilium regale*, the poetry of St John of the Cross. Then in September phlox, open-air incense, muffled nostalgia, of all garden plants the most English.

Among wild flowers four favourites – agrimony, elder and

meadow-sweet, those smells of summer, and artemisia or worm-
wood, autumn bitterness. And oh, the primroses and the blue-
bells! (Aldbourne)

‡ The olive and the plane are the trees that I prefer to all others
and I would always go a long way to see a fine one. Spanish olive
trees rarely grow to any great size because they are pruned and
not irrigated, so if one wishes to see fine and ancient trees one
must go to Italy or Greece. In Italy they grow well on the coasts
of Campania and Calabria, for example between Cape Palinuro
and Sapri, but the *locus classicus* for them is between Gioia Tauro
and Cittanova in the Calabrian toe. Here, in the valley of the
ancient Metaurus, in which Orestes bathed to purify himself of
his guilt, they grow in the form of popular trees, tall and tapering,
and are said to produce excellent fruit. All around, on the neigh-
bouring hill-slopes and across the Aspromonte among the ruins
of Locri, they preserve their usual spreading shape, but are of
great size and age. The most northern place in Europe where the
olive tree will grow freely is on the peninsula of Sirmione on
Lake Garda. As Tennyson wrote, 'Sweet Catullus's all-but-island,
olive-silvery Sirmio!'

There are fine and ancient olive trees in many parts of Greece
and the best eating olives in the world come from Kalamai in the
Peloponnese. But for beauty the great forest of these trees above
Mitylene, sloping down to the bottle-shaped Gulf of Geras, exceeds
anything that I know. One may walk in it for an hour or more
among the rocks and boulders that rise among the trunks of the
trees.

The finest plane trees I have seen are in Greece. The tallest
grow in the forests that cover the north of Euboea, but the most
gigantic grow on the slopes of Mount Pelion above Volos and
especially at Portaria and Makrinitsa. Here one tree will shade an
entire square, and so huge are their trunks that small rooms are
sometimes cut out in them. In western Turkey there are also fine
ones: it will be remembered from Herodotus that Xerxes, when
on his road to Sardes, admired one of them so much that he
presented it with golden ornaments and put it in the care of one
of his Immortals.

Other trees that I especially love are the cork oak and the Aleppo
pine. The former is at its best on the hills above Algeciras and in

the Sierra de Aracena near Huelva, though it also grows on the Massif des Maures on the French Riviera, while the latter is well seen when planted round farm houses in Languedoc. Its great bushy branches raised on red trunks give a nobility to the whole landscape.

Places & peoples

‡ *London in 1924* (from a letter). Yesterday, Sunday, I went to
Mile End. On my way there people were singing hymn tunes. In
Trafalgar Square a crowd had collected to hear the church bells
peal 'Abide with me' – one simply could not get away from
Jesus.

I wandered for two hours in the crowded streets off Aldgate,
listening to conjurers and athletes and preachers. A charming
negro, very politely dressed, was trying with the air of Jesus Christ
blessing the children to persuade a circle of diseased and ugly
human beings to buy his powdered galingale. A little taken every
night 'secured the functioning of the alimentary system, kept off
syphilis and brought Peace and Salvation'. No one bought any
except myself, moved by a sudden sympathy. He complained of
his audience – 'Now every time I discourse to you I tell you
something new, I do; I think of something fresh to say, light and
amusing, and especially instructive to creatures lost in ignorance
like yourselves. And yet how do you receive my blessed words of
help and light? What thought or care do you take of your salvation?'
Here he turned away and chewed vigorously. 'No, you merely
say – go to the devil with your salvation. I can't go on preaching
to you all the time, I can't go on telling you every day to save
your souls and bodies. I begin to get tired. I commence to weary
of your blindness. Yes – I do.'

The Jews were keeping Passover and a fat puffy woman, standing
on a stool, harangued them in a frightened mechanical voice –
telling them that the second Passover was better than the first for
the reason that 'God goes better every time'.

'Now come and wash in the Blood, O poor Lost Creatures.
Now then, come and wash in the Blood, in the Blood of the Most

Precious Lamb. That's it, boys, hang on to the Blood of the Lamb.'

Of all the thousands of faces I peered at I saw only one that did not seem to me bestial and repulsive, and that was the negro's. The rest were fit only for nightmares.

One I saw who was so incredibly repulsive that I shall never forget him. He was a racing tout collecting subscriptions. One saw only his mouth and hair and nostrils and neck, for over his eyes he wore a black mask. His bright red chin and red neck as full of folds as a bloodhound's had their outlet in a mouth as large as a bull's head, shapeless and in perpetual fleshy movement. Within it one saw a bluish tongue quivering like the organ of a new, obscene species, and rows of carious teeth jutted out of the blackness. His voice was a horror.

‡ *Paris.* I like the grey, serious sky, the tall, shuttered houses with their steep roofs and high windows that look as if they were thinking. And in the street one sees the objects they are thinking about – the bookshops with their fresh yellow paperbacks, the art shops and the antique shops with their gay window-shows, the picture galleries. And then the Seine, coiling like a snake through the great, spread-out city.

‡ Both the French and the Athenians have been great educators who helped to civilize the peoples with whom they came in contact. The French taught style, the Greeks form, and both had languages that were clear and precise and thus well fitted to express thoughts and ideas. But, compared to the Greeks, the French lack breadth of mind and imagination.

‡ When one says Europe one means France. All the other peoples of that continent have a tinge of provinciality. France is the norm.

‡ Descartes gave its form to the French mind as Malherbe did to its literature. It is a mind that is more prone to abstract ideas and to economy of expression than it is to conformity to reality. This

helps to give every Frenchman a respect for intelligence which the
English, who are equally intelligent, lack. Yet the French are
supreme in all the arts of life, except those English ones of ease
and comfort.

‡ What astonishes and delights in Italy is the explosion of great
architecture that bursts out of the soil in every small town and
city. No people has ever built so lavishly or with such show and
magnificence unless it was the ancient Greeks, who like the Italians
were possessed of great civic pride which made their city-states
compete fiercely with one another. Far wealthier states have arisen
since then, but what have they done to prove their worth to
posterity?

‡ When one travels far enough one travels in time as well as in
space. Those people who fell in love with Spain before 1930 were
not only drawn by its Spanishness but by the fact that it belonged
to the pre-industrial age. Anyone who visited Morocco at that
time was not only seeing the East but was reliving the early Middle
Ages.

‡ What most delights the traveller from northern Europe as he
makes his way through Spain is its emptiness. Bare mountain
ranges, bone-coloured rocks and hills, flat heaths and *páramos*,
hardly a house. And then suddenly a pool of greenery and a white
village. In such a country one can breathe.

‡ When someone from the north of Europe says 'Spain' he usually
means Andalusia, whereas a Spaniard means first his own province
and then Castile.

‡ The Spaniards are an emphatic, positive-minded people who
tend to hold their opinions strongly. They are very social by
nature – indeed their attention is so entirely focussed on the human
scene that they have few thoughts to spare for anything outside
it. Their tastes incline them to the concrete and they show little
bent for abstract ideas. Thus there has never been a Spanish

scientist or mathematician of any eminence, and if they have good technicians, engineers and doctors that is because these professions serve the interests of society. However their special quality would seem to lie in their being more deeply planted than other people in their own lives and personalities. This could be called egoism, but it does not prevent them from having warm and kindly feelings for others because they recognize that they have the same right to self-assertion as themselves. They are a people who fulfil themselves best in action, as their astounding exploits in the conquest and exploration of America show, but their energies are today muffled because to release them they need an opening that appeals to their imagination and offers them full scope as individuals or as members of a band. At bottom they are anarchists, tamed by the strong social pressures they live under, and for that reason bad organizers and unprofessional in their attitude to work. At present they are going through the process of being acclimatized to the disciplines (as well as to the rewards) of industrial life and of parliamentary democracy.

‡ Spaniards are better integrated in life than other peoples. One feels as one watches them that they are conscious all the time and in a very satisfying way of their own existence and identity. Indeed they sometimes seem to live in a bath of themselves. Then every Spaniard is like a man-of-war, armed cap-à-pie to defend himself. That is why so much restraint and good manners are necessary. One man-of-war must reassure the other man-of-war that its guns will not be wanted.

‡ Their religion with its Virgin Mother and its sacred Child provides the sanction for their family life. The teachings of Jesus, the doctrines of the Incarnation and Atonement mean little to them and in the Crucifixion it is usually the sorrow of the Mother that is emphasized rather than the death of the Son. For the Holy Family is a projection of the Mediterranean ideal into the sky, and the dubious role of Joseph emphasizes the irrelevance, from the woman's point of view, of the man and the poor view taken by them of sex.

‡ There is no country where love is taken more idealistically than it is in Spain. Calderon expresses that sentiment when he says 'Alma en mí ha sido mi amor' – 'My love has been a property of my soul.' There has never been a time when Spaniards married for anything else.

‡ Spaniards adore their children to the point where they like even their destructiveness. When Pepe, aged five, throws the crockery on the floor they say, 'What a little man!'

‡ An old peasant said to me: 'They say it's the same sun you see all the world over, but I shouldn't be surprised if there were two.'

‡ As they sit at their tables outside the cafés their eyes record as on a photographic plate the people who are passing, but on a deeper level they are listening to themselves living.

‡ There is a negativity in the Spanish mind, a capacity for emptying itself of both thought and feeling, that makes them given to turning it outwards and seeking stimulus in the spectacle of other people. In the street, in bars, wherever they are sitting or standing, they are watching the passers-by and passively recording their features. It is not that they are bored, for Spaniards are too absorbed in their own existence to know the meaning of boredom – they are merely whiling their time away. Thus the traveller is always aware, wherever he goes, of eyes blankly fixed on him.

‡ The conversation of Spanish peasants has always been noted for its sententiousness. In their tight community life they keep their eyes open and turn things over in their minds, and as they grow older they take to philosophizing about them. In every Spanish countryman there is a little Seneca – hence the large numbers of *refranes* or proverbs that they use. But proverbs are the creation of a people who cannot read – a stock of wise sayings that teach the art of life – so that today they are falling out of use because school education is taking their place.

‡ Spaniards are very little interested in other countries and rarely travel abroad for pleasure except to Paris or Rome. But they are intensely interested in what foreigners say of them because, with the Civil War fresh in their minds, they are going through a phase of self-examination to discover what sort of people they are. Thus no book has had a wider circulation in recent years than one (a very brilliant one) on the vices of the Spanish people. But if they are so taken up with the peculiarities of their countrymen, they are on another and deeper level concerned with their *patria chica*. Every large *pueblo* can command the loyalty of its inhabitants, while the competition between provincial capitals as to which has the finest Easter processions or the best football team can arouse wild enthusiasm. This pride in their own region spreads over onto other things. To give an example, I have a botanist friend who has written a useful book on the flora of Malaga. One day I showed him a rare plant which excited him greatly, but when I told him that I had found it two kilometres beyond the boundary of the province, he lost all interest in it.

‡ The intense love of Spaniards for their native *pueblo* is shown in the large number of popular *coplas* or verses that, till the transistor radio came in, were sung all over Spain in the fields and in cafés in the style known as *cante jondo*. Here is an example:

> Sanlúcar de Barrameda,
> Quién te pudiera traer
> Metido en la faltriquera
> como un pliego de papel!

Sanlúcar de Barrameda, would I could carry you folded up in my pocket like a piece of paper!

‡ The great quality of Spaniards is their vitality. This is not a surface vitality like that of the Neapolitans, but involves their whole nature. It makes them a pleasant people to live among.

‡ García Lorca said that a dead Spaniard is more dead than anyone else. This is because he had more life to lose.

‡ Spaniards have always had the reputation for having more pride than other people. This is still true though they rarely display it, but it makes them susceptible. Their manners are so easy, frank and natural that a foreigner may easily forget this and offend them by seeming to treat them too casually. Those who have most pride of all are the *gitanos* or gypsies.

‡ Well-to-do Spaniards tend to live more for show than for pleasure. In their cars, in their houses, in their parties and entertainments they provide good examples of conspicuous consumption. The working classes resemble them in this and will spend their money on expensive clothes for their small children rather than on better food. 'What will people say?' is always at the back of their minds.

‡ Spaniards are great promisers, but one must never rely on their offers of help unless they are close friends, because these are merely expressions of good intentions and are not meant to be taken literally.

‡ If one wishes to understand Spain one should read the novels of Pérez Galdós. No writer has ever portrayed his country better, and he is as good on the poor as on the middle classes. Little has changed in the Spanish character since his time except that religious fanaticism has worked itself out and politics has taken its place.

‡ There is a stronger feeling for family privacy in Spain than in any other European country except Greece and Sicily. One can be a good friend of a Spaniard for many years without ever being invited into his house. This is often said to be the Moorish influence, but in reality it is just a characteristic of Mediterranean peoples. Men meet their friends in clubs or cafés and women meet at bazaars or sewing parties organized by the Church. That at least has been the custom until recently, but today husbands and wives go about much more frequently together and on Sundays link up with their friends at popular restaurants. Still the feeling for family privacy remains strong in other ways, and in the biographies of dead

writers or politicians great circumspection has to be shown in referring to the fact that they had mistresses, even when they were not married. Very few volumes of letters are published in Spain, and never love-letters.

‡ The unsocial man is rare in Spain. Almost all Spaniards are gregarious. Besides it is important for a man of the middle classes to have friends since it is through them that he gets jobs and commissions. A man who is *simpático* can go far. Yet under social and family life there is another level, which is that of the solitary *Yo* or individual. Many Spaniards are intensely conscious of this and of their essential loneliness as human beings. That is what once made Spain the most religious country in Europe and is no doubt what leads to so much poetry being read and written today. Every city has its group of poets and often its poetry magazine and printing press as well.

‡ The Spaniards are nearer in disposition to the ancient Greeks and Romans than to any modern people because they have preserved so much of that fine balance of the senses and the intellect which the Romans called *humanitas*. But they have added to this Mediterranean quality something stubborn and continental, as when the tablelands of Castile come down to meet the pine and the olive. Its taste is sometimes heavy and ponderous and sometimes sharp and acrid.

‡ Much of what travellers have written about the Spanish character must be taken back now that from being natives of a poor and undeveloped country they have become those of a prosperous and busy one. With the passing of those ways and customs that went with a leisurely life they have lost much of their old idiosyncrasy and drawn closer in their mode of life to other European peoples, just as their towns, now surrounded by ugly blocks of modern-style buildings, have lost much of their former charm. Underneath no doubt they remain much the same, but on the surface the change has been great since money and money-making have assumed a role they did not have before.

‡ 'A saying at Avila – "It is the custom." How much respect did these grave, disillusioned, limited people of Avila have for their customs, and in particular for their religion? Not much I think, at bottom; but nothing else was practically within their range; and if something else had been possible for them, would it have been better? The more intelligent of them would have doubted this and resigned themselves to the daily round. What they had and what they thought were at least "the custom"; they could live and express themselves on those assumptions. Their inner man, in bowing to usage, could preserve his dignity. In breaking away, as the demagogues and cheap intellectuals wished them to do, they would have fallen into mental confusion and moral anarchy. Their lives would have been no better, and their judgements much worse' (Santayana, *Persons and Places*).

This is the picture of a Spain which no longer exists.

‡ Once many years ago I got into conversation with a very poor man from Almeria who in his youth had been a sailor. He told me that he knew my country for he had spent a year working in the docks at Liverpool. 'And how did you like it?' I asked. 'Did the climate depress you?' 'The climate was all right,' he answered. 'Plenty of nice rain. And Liverpool is a very fine city. Only I was always hungry. I could not get used to the taste of horse-flesh, so when I wanted to fill my stomach I tried the bread. But this didn't help much for your bread is not nourishing like ours. It leaves one empty. Never mind, I've often been hungry before. But what I couldn't get over were the bedbugs. They ate one alive.'

Now Almeria and all the villages round it were overrun with bedbugs and except in the big hotel, which I could not afford, it was hard to find a room without them. But the English ones, it seemed, were worse. This was many years before George Orwell wrote *The Road to Wigan Pier*, and I realized that I did not know my own country. I had had to come to Spain to learn about it.

‡ In travel we meet the kind of people we would run a mile to avoid in our own country. The pleasure of listening to and speaking a foreign language prevents them from boring us. Everything they say seems fresh and interesting because the words they employ are new and we too feel inspired as poets when in a happy

moment we pour out a few commonplace phrases. This is one of
the things that makes travel so stimulating, while another is that
when we meet one of our compatriots we see him with a different
and perhaps more critical eye. One must go abroad if one wishes
to see one's own country in perspective.

‡ The United States is a country where the compressed gases of
Europe have been released and have then expanded suddenly to
fill a vast, half-empty region. This has created a climate of euphoria
and optimism as well as much goodwill and friendliness, but
operating in a vacuum with no historical background to channel
it. Except in some corners of the South there is little feeling for
place, home or material possessions in spite of many attempts in
the past to create them. The landscape is too continental to en-
courage the putting down of roots and the pressures that make
for a continual change of habitat are too many.

‡ The US is a country founded on an idea, which was once that
of liberty and freedom from oppression, but is today that of a high
living-standard for all those who are sufficiently energetic and
able. It shows how the ideals of the French Enlightenment work
out in a setting where there are no traditions to hamper them, and
no restraints on the power of the individual to rise and better
himself. As has often been said, every poor immigrant carries a
millionaire's cheque book in his pack. This means that the attach-
ment of Americans to their native country is based more on their
loyalty to an idea than, as it is in Europe, to their love for soil
and environment. Yet, since Christian compassion does not form
part of this idea, there is nothing in their system to prevent the
weaker from going to the wall. This is a country that worships
success and despises failure. Money alone counts, because it is the
one status symbol.

‡ In the United States the rich think it an eccentricity if a friend
or relative of theirs is poor: he hasn't got the money, they say,
because he doesn't want it. It's like being a vegetarian.

‡ According to Alvin Toffler in his prophetic book *Future Shock* the variety of life styles in the United States is rapidly increasing. All traditional values, except in small local pockets, are dying out. The past being a blank sheet, new social and sexual mores are continually being introduced, such as, for example, 'swinging' or wife-swapping. America is thus getting to be a gigantic laboratory, both for new technical inventions and for new modes of living, while an increasingly large part of the population is learning to be mobile, ready at any moment to pack up like nomads and migrate a thousand miles or so to richer pastures.

To most Europeans who have read Toffler's book this will seem an unacceptable way of living. If they concur with what he says they will see their American cousins as a people who have no roots in the past, sprung suddenly out of the earth like dragons' teeth and floating on the surface of life in a way that precludes their having access to any of its deeper sources: restless because their eyes are fixed on the future – that wonderful future where man, thanks to his new discoveries in biochemistry, will live to the age of Methuselah and be as powerful as the gods. Yet although it is their belief that scientific techniques can achieve anything which gives the Americans their optimism, as individuals they are basically less sure of themselves than are Europeans or Orientals, who have the rheumatism of tradition in their bones with all its impediments and all its fortifying resources. They feel when they reflect on it a certain brittleness in their situation because they are uncomfortably aware of lacking something that the older races possess, and besides, are filled with doubts and misgivings as to whether, living in a dangerous and unpredictable world, they will ever be allowed to attain their promised land. For the course which they pursue with such energy and dynamism is one in which all the values are material, although in fact they show no respect for matter. As soon as any object they have made has been used, it is scrapped so that something better may take its place. Thus a skyscraper that was put up only twenty years ago will be pulled down to give place to a taller one. That is to say that they are as nomadic in time as in space, for with every generation they change their social structure so that even the ashes of their camp-fires are buried under the sand.

‡ America is famous for its aggressiveness and violence. More murders are committed each year in the one state of Texas than in the whole of Europe outside Ulster. Various reasons have been given for this – the old frontier mentality, the colour question, the ghettos where the poor live, and the drug habit, but among the prosperous middle classes there is also a violence of a Hemingway kind, due, it is said, to doubts about their manhood and to a wish to assert it. Drink brings it out, for the Americans are more given than almost any other people to alcoholism. But what strikes Europeans about what one may call the raw Americans they meet is their naïveté and lack of sophistication. Unless they have lived for some time in Europe or in the East they show an extraordinary innocence, and this, though it was a quality admired by Henry James, puts them at a disadvantage. They have not, like the members of older civilizations, been passed through the fires of history, so that there are many things that they do not understand. One of these is irony, which in their eyes is a sign of treachery to the great American ideal of faith in human nature and its future. They would like to be the leaders of the world, not from a craving for power but in order to carry their ideal to other nations (as well as to secure an easy access to raw materials), but they are handicapped in this by their lack of an imaginative understanding of foreign peoples or races. Yet, if they lack maturity, they have several admirable qualities which are badly needed in the world today – energy, goodwill and generosity.

‡ What holds this vast country together and keeps it on a straight course is the power and liberalism of its national press, just as broadcasting and television are the enlightening influence in Britain, though not always its moral one.

‡ Henry James said that the only good European was the American who had taken up his residence there. The rest were Frenchmen, Englishmen, Italians, and so forth. And it is true that these Americans are almost the only people in the West who do not have something provincial about them. They are the truly civilized and sophisticated in the widest sense of those terms.

‡ Of the two sexes in the United States the women are usually those who impress Europeans the most. Henry James made the American girl famous, and they are still outstanding for their beauty, frankness of manner and independence of character. But one's American friends tell one that they compete actively with the men, both at college and after, and that when they marry they are apt to take over the reins and rule the house, which it is the easier to do because the husband is absent at his office. Then as mothers they tend to dominate their sons, which is no doubt the reason why so many of the American men one meets show a strange softness and spinelessness. This strikes one as paradoxical in members of a nation which is outstanding in its energy, just as one is surprised to meet well-placed Soviet Russians who show none of the qualities for which their novelists have made them famous, but are pure cyphers. But then one remembers that it is today the corporations with their streamlined bureaucracies that run the States, while Lenin and Stalin have seen to it that no outstanding personalities can raise their heads in Russia.

But do these generalizations about peoples and countries lead one anywhere? There are so many exceptions.

Introspection

‡ I am lying on my bed, my eyes closed, listening to the sound of children calling, dogs barking, horses trotting, goats pitter-pattering in the bright sunlight. The climate of Malaga gives me this pure distilled pleasure of being sleepily alive.

‡ There is nothing more nostalgic in this country than the nasal voice of the lottery seller moving down a hot village street. It takes me back to the time when I first came to Spain forty years ago and street criers were more common. Sounds and smells, how keenly they have the property of preserving, like flies in amber, little fragments of one's past which sight, being a more exploited sense, is unable to do!

‡ A distant memory has just come back to me. Walking one day by the river my mother asked me, 'What profession do you mean to take up when you leave school?' I did not answer, but I thought, 'A tramp'.

‡ 'Ainsi ne traçai-je de moi, dit Ménélaque, que la plus vague et la plus incertaine figure, à force de ne la vouloir pas limiter.' 'Thus I traced out for my character only the vaguest and most hazy outline, because I did not want to limit it' (André Gide, *Nourritures terrestres*). This recalls the plan I made for myself as a young man at Yegen for keeping the pores of my mind open and not crystallizing or growing a mask or shell. I must disown no part of myself.

‡ Rain, rain, rain. It brings out all the scents – roses, heliotrope, lemon leaves, loquat flowers, freesias, but subduing them a little and mixing them with the smell of the wet earth. This garden is where I should like to live if I were blind, because in its soft air the sounds as well as the scents have a soothing and memory-provoking quality. Ordinarily the senses take in too much. One would better enjoy using one's eyes if they recorded fewer things, because the less clearly objects are defined, the greater is the charge of emotional associations they carry. One might say that the chief aesthetic discovery of this age has been the importance of the half-seen and half-understood, though the critics of poetry try to destroy this for us by discussing and 'explicating', as they call it, every line.

‡ Since my strongest feeling in literature has been for language, what I have most valued in both poetry and prose has been the texture. In my own books I have put this before everything else, neglecting the prime need for a good general arrangement. In my novels this haphazard treatment of the plot has been fatal. As I wrote I poured in more and more characters and scenes because life excited me, when I should have studied Homer's *Iliad* and the Greek dramatists and learned from them the supreme importance of form.

‡ When I look back on my literary career I see that I have done well on subjects for which I had no special gift or preparation, but less well on those to which I felt that my talent and mode of feeling naturally inclined me. Can it be that I am a poet manqué, whose poetic instincts are always trying to break out in a medium that is not suited to them? Thus my last novel *The Lighthouse Always Says Yes* is a poor affair, yet it has a scene on flamenco dancing in Seville that would stand out in any prose anthology.

‡ I see my mind as a large hall or theatre, all dark, in which someone is wandering about with a candle. Often only one subject can be picked out at a time, but as the candle moves one or two others become momentarily connected. At very long intervals an electric light is turned on and a considerable part of the furniture

and decoration becomes visible, but before these can be properly examined the light has gone out again. (1960)

‡ Every morning I would wake up feeling that I knew nothing. This sense of my ignorance, dullness, feebleness of mind could be crushing and only left me when I sat down to work. Then something happened. Out of the dullness words and thoughts surged up and I found that I had things to say. But where did they come from?

‡ On reading two highly favourable reviews of my history of Spanish literature and getting a letter from Roman Carande, the eminent Spanish economist and historian, praising my *Spanish Labyrinth*, I ask myself – who is this person who writes these books that are said to be so admirable both in sense and style? Certainly not the 'I' whom I see when I look into myself, that vague, floating, ever-changing entity who lives in a blur of poor memories and muddled impressions. I feel like a table which has come to see itself through the eyes of an atomic physicist as a sort of emptiness with little points of energy darting about haphazardly in it, and then discovers that other people regard it as a solid object with fixed dimensions.

‡ The mind has its phases as the sea has its tides. Take as an image of it an estuary on the Breton coast. At high tide there is water everywhere and sailing boats skim its surface, but at low tide rocks and shoals appear and the waves break round them. These are the fears and doubts that affect us in our low moods but which will vanish when the tide returns. Most depressions and neuroses are due to a draining away of psychic energy and if the waters of the mind can be persuaded to rise again, our boat will sail safely over them without the help of a psychiatrist.

‡ We are often frustratingly aware that our consciousness has a frontier beyond which we cannot penetrate. Yet something is going on there – there are little hills and trees and moving figures dimly glimpsed through the fog. It is only through our intuitions that we can have momentary access to them.

‡ Sometimes when I run over in my mind the different feelings I have had during a single evening I feel that I must be crazy. I meet and talk to a French gas-fitter in a bar. I like his conversation and think that I must arrange in my next incarnation to be a French workman as he is. Then I go to a performance of Indian ballet and am so carried away that I regret that my father was not an Indian Brahmin so that I could have learned those temple dances and belonged to a polytheistic religion where the generative process is deified. But no, I think as I walk home, India is not a country for me: the only polytheism I like is the Greek one. They created the greatest civilization the world has seen, and yet how simple and unsophisticated we should find them if we could meet them today, for they were a people entirely lacking in self-consciousness. Better to be what I am, a modern writer. Then before going to bed I glance at the manuscript I am working on to see how it reads and am shocked to find how bad it is and all my other books along with it. Indeed, I say to myself, I made a great mistake in choosing a literary career. I should have been a mining prospector, one of those tough guys who knock about the world and are in touch in the hard way with life and Nature. It is not till next morning at breakfast that I feel glad that the chains of habit that bind me to my niche in the world are so strong, for where should I be otherwise? I hurry off to my room to start a new paragraph.

‡ In old age we learn to draw in our frontiers. Desire fails, the grasshopper becomes a burden, the knees weaken, the memory decays, yet somewhere underneath there is the little boy who once ran racing over the fields and saw the sorrel glowing like a flame in the grass as the last rays of the sun fell slantingly upon it. Just as the stump of an old tree can still put out new shoots, so the mind and heart can still recall past memories and, what is more, generate fresh thoughts and feelings. But the greatest change lies in the falling off of egoism because, since this ego is about to flicker out and disappear, there is no longer any reason for cherishing it so lovingly. And then our eyes are opened and we see the world for what it is – a place of savagery and cruelty where men behave worse than wild beasts, and in the name of what they call their ideals, which are really their cravings for power and influence, destroy and eat one another. This is the moment to shut the

history books that tell of men's crimes towards one another and to turn to poetry and painting, to dance and music, which remind us that men are also capable of enthralment and delight, and that life has its good moments as well as its horrors and its shambles.

Dreams

‡   A charm against nightmares:

Procul, o procul uagantum
portenta somniorum!
procul esto peruicaci
praestigiator astu!

O tortuose serpens,
qui mille per meandros
fraudesque flexuosas
agitas quieta corda,

discede...

Be far, oh far from us, you monsters of our disordered
dreams! Be far from us, demon, with your subtle decep-
tions! Depart, O tortuous serpent, who with a thousand
coils and subtle frauds agitates our peaceful hearts!
(Prudentius (348–c. 420), *A Hymn Before Sleep*)

‡ Dreams are like landscapes. When one wakes up they are all
around us, and one has to move a certain distance away from them
to see what they are.

‡ However extraordinary anything that happens to us in a dream
may be, we are never surprised by it. That is because, since dreams
form a self-enclosed world impervious to rational criticism, we
can never judge them by the rules that apply in real life.

‡ We forget our dreams, not because they contain material that something in us wishes to suppress, but for the same reason that we forget telephone numbers. They have not been incorporated into the causal sequence of our lives.

‡ If, as Freud asserts, the obscurity and incoherence of dreams are due to their real meaning having been distorted by a 'censor' who wishes to prevent us from understanding them, how is it that we sometimes have dreams of a very shocking and disturbing kind which have not been censored at all? To give an example, a friend of mine dreamed in the most vivid and circumstantial way that he was copulating with his mother, and awoke with a feeling of deep horror. Of what use, one may ask, would a censor be if he could allow such dreams to pass without disguising them?

‡ The great thing about dreams is that you can always get out of them. Thus if you happen to be standing on the summit of Mount Kanchenjunga and are all alone and have lost your ice-pick and night is coming on and a thick mist has blown up, there is no need to feel alarmed. You have only to open your eyes to be back in your bed.

‡ We only know the ends of our dreams, never the beginnings. When they come out of their hiding-places they leave their spoors behind them.

‡ If one lies in the sun in a dreamy mood and lets one's thoughts take their course, it often happens that a train of images will pass in rapid succession through the mind. Sometimes there will be perceptible traces of association between these images, but often they will be so faint that the process will appear to be a random one. The reason for this would seem to be that, whereas in normal waking states there is a current of mind which excludes all associations that are not required by it, in dreamy and relaxed moods there is no such current. Then one passes into a doze and finally into a true sleep in which the dramatic faculty of dreaming makes its appearance. Yet the more or less casual associations still persist

and by diverting it help to give it its waywardness and unintelligibility. That is to say, a dream is a discharge of energy making its way through the confused and irrational elements of the subconscious, some of which it absorbs into itself, but always seeking to fulfil its purpose, whatever that may be. No censor is required to twist its meaning, though of course, as in waking life, there may be one.

‡ Since the consciousness is that part of the mind where the attention is focussed upon the matter in hand, it naturally excludes everything that is not relevant to its purpose. It can only function by concentrating.

‡ It is immediately after awaking from a dream that the mind, puzzled by the confused dream material and wishing to give some comprehensible shape to it, shows itself during half a minute or so at its most creative. One can perhaps compare this state to the 'nascent' condition in which a chemical element finds itself on its release from molecular union with another element and so aroused that it is able to form a second union with one of those inert elements which are not usually combinable with it. This state of nascency, as it is called, is analogous to that into which poets fall when they are composing a poem. They have escaped through a sudden access of energy from the world of habit in which words have only their useful, everyday meanings and are free to explore a field in which wider associations and combinations are open to them.

‡ There are relations and categories in dreams which cannot be described in words or made intelligible to the conscious mind, but which are yet perfectly intelligible to the dreamer. This raises questions about the processes of thinking in the primitive mind and in the minds of animals, where speech has not yet frozen thought into fixed grammatical and logical forms.

‡ Consciousness is like a well-lit stage. The actors who have learned their parts will come on when they hear their cue, but all

the time thousands of others are waiting and whispering in the wings.

‡ It seems probable that the same mental activities that one observes in dreaming are present in the subconscious layers of the mind during waking states, but are not perceived, for the same reason that the stars are invisible during daylight. According to Jung an idea passes from the subconscious to the conscious when it acquires an extra dose of energy.

‡ Some dreams carry with them a special feeling-tone – sweet, strange, penetrating, frequently erotic – that is unlike anything we experience in waking life and which may continue to affect us for several days after. If we could have such dreams every night we would prefer sleeping to waking, yet the psychoanalysts never allude to this property. Like old-fashioned critics of painting they are only interested in the representational or meaningful content of the dreams they analyse and neglect their emotive quality. There are, I believe, some traces in literature of this strange feeling-tone that only dreams convey, for example in *Le Grand Meaulnes*, in Gérard de Nerval's *Sylvie*, in the first part of the *Roman de la Rose*, in Kafka's *Castle*, in the best of St John of the Cross's poems, in Donne's *Hymn to God My God in My Sickness* and perhaps in some passages of Shelley's *The Triumph of Life*. And of course in a very different way in *Alice in Wonderland*, which consciously draws on dream mechanics, but has no feeling-tone.

‡ Our dreams sometimes tell us, in a quite simple and direct way, about our past. Thus they will reveal to us the worries and anxieties which we have suffered from at various periods of our lives and which have been forgotten because they have been overlaid by other more concrete memories. By reviving the actual feeling of those times they re-create the past for us in a way which our more factual recollections fail to do.

‡ Some dreams throw a satirical light on the present. Thus we can have dreams that parody our own behaviour. We see ourselves

coming into a room, greeting the people in it with an effusive smile, talking hard to prevent them from getting in a word, forgetting to ask them about their own affairs, seizing any opportunity for boasting or showing off, dropping out of the conversation when it does not interest us, slipping in something malicious about an absent friend – that is to say, putting into operation all the self-asserting and self-protecting mechanisms of what we call social life. For it would seem that inside us there is always a critical and ironic eye watching how we behave, which implies that we are not quite so dense and insensitive as we appear to be.

‡ There can be puns in dreams. The other night, for example, I dreamed of a card game I was playing and which was called Job. When I woke up I saw that it was patience.

‡ When one smokes hashish one's sensibility to forms, colours and above all to music is increased. A peculiar significance attaches itself to everything that one sees and hears, so that one is content to live in the present, attuned to one's surroundings and at peace with oneself. One doesn't think, but is merely blissfully aware. But when one eats the drug in its pure form the effect is very different – indeed the opposite. Vivid images pour through the mind in rapid succession and one has no power to arrest or to control them, but is completely under their spell. At the same time one is aware that each of these images has links or associations stretching out through the whole of one's conscious mind which are far more subtle than any that one had perceived before, so that if one could follow them up one would make the most surprising discoveries which would enlarge one's view of the world very considerably by showing one the hidden correspondences that lie in things. The range of analogies offered would make those in Donne's poems seem child's play. Only one cannot follow them up, one cannot stop for long enough to do this, because a fresh image has now appeared to engage one's attention, and then another after it. Yet if one dictates what one is given time to dictate to a companion – some of these subtle and illuminating associations and connections, some of these jokes that seem at the time so full of wit and profundity – and then reads them next day, one finds that their point and meaning have totally evaporated. Either one's

perceptions were so sharpened and refined when under the influence of the drug that one's normal ones are too coarse to follow them, or the whole thing is an illusion. Perhaps what one learns best from this experiment of hashish-eating is that the mind is most adjusted to reality when it moves with a certain slowness and deliberation. Time must be given to allow us to digest our new impressions.

‡ All through my life I have dreamed a great deal of landscapes. Since Nature has meant much to me, these dreams have usually been happy ones and when on occasion they were of picking wild flowers they were ecstatic, because flowers are for me promises of happiness. Many of these landscapes have recurred in dream after dream, giving me the strange feeling that I had seen them before, perhaps in some previous existence. A few of them appear to derive from places I visited as a small boy, but most are of composite origin. What is curious is that I have never dreamed of the First World War, in which I was involved for more than two years. Its horrors and its terrors seem to have left no trace behind them.

‡ Dreams can have a beauty or an oddity that have little to do with their interpretation. Since I used to have many dreams of this sort I will give a few of them here solely for the sake of their literary quality, just as I might offer a string of short poems. Most of them have little or no bearing on my life because they are end-pieces to dreams, composed as I was in the process of awaking, whereas others are complete dreams. I wrote them down immediately on a pad I kept by my side and I have not in any way improved on them.

‡ I dreamed that I was a white hare leaping through a dark forest. Following a narrow path I came to the edge of the trees and saw the stars showing through a rift in the clouds. I saw one particular constellation, then raced back under the trees. (1916)

This was a very moving dream and has always been very important to me because it showed that the hare was my totem animal. I too lived by flight and escape.

‡ I dreamed that we were like frogs in a pond. We sank into the water, which was our private world, to think and sleep, but came to the surface to croak and communicate. When I awoke from my dream I heard the cocks crowing from the distance and realized that they were the barometer of my happiness. (1916)

‡ At about this time I had a dream in which I saw a toad which was being attacked by a dog. It lifted its paws in vain for it had no strength with which to defend itself. This dream filled me, and still fills me today, with intense pity and horror. If only it had been able either to run or to fight back!

‡ I dreamed that I was in the country of distant things, where cocks crow, voices of children call, suns set. I was there, yet they had not changed, but were still distant. (1932)

‡ I dreamed of tall blocks of flats or skyscrapers in which the floors were rented according to the intellectual energy of the occupants, the most intelligent being on the top. I myself lived in the lift. (1932)

‡ I dreamed that I was lying beside a girl of fifteen, my sister, on a bed. Realization of how enormously the pleasure of making love was increased because it was forbidden. (I have never had a sister.)

‡ I dreamed that I looked into a mirror and saw myself and the other people who were with me doing things that in fact we were not doing. Did the mirror reflect the past or the future, or our secret desires, or what?

‡ My young daughter Miranda had woken me several times by calling out in her sleep and then I dreamed this. Her cries in the night were prophetic and foretold the future. But these cries were affected by what we gave her to eat. Therefore by choosing her diet I could control the future.

‡ I dreamed that I was writing a science-fiction novel, cast for the year 2000. Artificial planets had long been established and visits to space a hundred miles above the earth's surface were a tourist attraction. An American Burial Society had some time before this contracted to shoot up corpses by rocket to a region where they would revolve perpetually, unchanged and uncorrupted, in an orbit round the earth. Coasting along the edge of this orbit in a tourist spaceship one could see the millions of the dead, sitting or reclining free in space. The more famous ones had uranium plaques giving their names, which detectors on the spaceship could pick out. (1944)

‡ I dreamed that I was in Algeria, living in a Kabyle village and perhaps a Kabyle myself. I began to write down what I was seeing and wrote this: 'But now Ouali was singing. People came up and stood around, but no one dared to speak or interrupt her, because if they had done so her song would have broken into little sharp pieces in the air which would have killed the children who were standing there when they breathed them in.'

I should add that I had recently returned from a trip through Algeria and had just read two novels by a Kabyle writer called Mouloud Mammeri.

‡ A dream of Bloomsbury. It was like a sky packed with ice-blue clouds. There was something cold and glittering about it. A lot of frozen conversation drifted down.

‡ I dreamed that I was asleep in a chair. My parents appeared behind me and wished to wake me, but they were surprisingly timid and patient, quite unlike what they would have been in real life. For they were aware that they were dead and so had reduced powers, and in fact would not have been able to appear in my presence if I had not been sleeping – that is, close to death.

‡ I went to bed feeling unwell. I realized that I had flu and my temperature went up to 101. Then I had a dream. I saw Mr Hollo-

way, an old man who had been a sailor and did odd jobs in gardens, standing at the kitchen door. In the insidiously threatening voice of all beggars he said to me, 'I would like to have a word with you.' He then led me out into the street. The frost was so hard that the houses were crackling under it like rivers in Siberia. The moon shone down on the thin snow. I noticed that he was coughing badly and all at once I began to feel very cold. Looking around me I saw that we had passed through the gate into the cemetery. 'You see this,' said Mr Holloway suddenly. And he swept his hand round over the gravestones and then pointed downwards. 'You see this. This is the True Hollow Way. Before much time has passed on that clock you will be meeting me down here.' His eyes, filmed over by cataract and lit by the moon, looked like two great raindrops gathering weight to fall, and as I woke I remembered that he had died only the previous week. (Aldbourne, January 1940)

‡ *A dream of death.* I dreamed I was walking down the street of a town I did not know. It seemed at first quite an ordinary little town, but when I came to look at it more closely I saw that it was less ordinary than I had supposed. First I was struck by the shops. Over a confectioner's there hung a sign that said 'Dental Confectionery' and in its window there was a row of chocolate skulls with real teeth set in them. Then I saw a photographer's studio which bore an announcement that it took photographs of young people which showed them as they would be when they were very old. 'That's a disagreeable idea,' I said to myself and turned into a shop that sold children's books. I was looking vaguely round it when the salesman came up to me and, taking in his hand one of those innocent-looking volumes, turned it upside down, and I saw that all the illustrations when seen in that way were of very old and decrepit people and that some of them, instead of faces, had skulls. 'Educative,' he remarked thoughtfully.

'And now look at this,' he said. 'Here is a book for more advanced children.' I opened it and saw on the title page a coloured plate of a woman giving birth to a very old man. The details were repulsive.

'Rather realistic,' he remarked. 'Now to change to something more fanciful, here we have a book of popular verse for teenagers. Some of them are quite pretty.'

Opening it at random, I read:

I thought I saw a pretty girl was ready for a kiss.
I looked again and saw it was a death's head on a stick.

And lower down:

I thought I saw a little girl a-riding on a bicycle.
I looked again and saw it was an Andes Inca icicle.

And I remembered that I had only the day before read an account of an Inca girl in Peru who had been found frozen in a glacier and was as perfectly preserved as when she had died a thousand years before.

'Don't show me any more,' I said, but as I left the shop I saw on the wall a card offering a prize for an essay on the subject 'Why is death so funny?'

'That's for the higher school grades,' the man said and, looking at him again, I saw that he now had a snowy white head and beard.

'My arctic dress,' he said. 'One must get ready for the expedition.'
(May 1944, just after my fiftieth birthday)

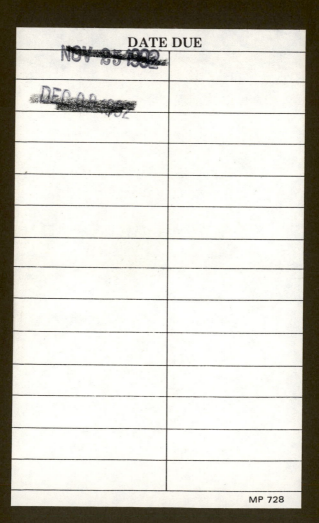